WORLD WAR II

DIVIDE & CONQUER

WORLD WAR II
DIVIDE & CONQUER

Published by Bookmart Ltd 2005

Blaby Road,
Wigson,
Leicester,
LE18 4SE
Books@bookmart.co.uk

All notations of errors or omissions (author inquiries, permissions) concerning the content of this book should be addressed to TAJ Books 27, Ferndown Gardens, Cobham, Surrey, UK, KT11 2BH, info@tajbooks.com.

ISBN 1-84509-168-X

Printed in China.
1 2 3 4 5 08 07 06 05

CONTENTS

Hitler accepts the ovation of the Reichstag after announcing the `peaceful' acquisition of Austria. It set the stage to annex the Czechoslovakian Sudetenland, largely inhabited by a German- speaking population.

By the 17th day after France's proclamation of general mobilisation, Poland's existence as an independent state had been destroyed for the next five and a half years. There had been no precedent for such a catastrophe since Napoleon's destruction of Prussia at Jena in 1806. It was the result not so much of Poland's military weaknesses at the crucial moment as of the matériel, numerical, and strategic superiority of the German Army and of the Luftwaffe, helped by the fatal mistakes of the Polish High Command.

Within the frontiers which had been laid down by the Treaty of Versailles, Marshal Rydz-Smigly and his commanders had a difficult problem in planning the defence of Poland against Hitler's rearmed Germany. A glance at the map will show the reason for this. From Suwalki, on the frontier between East Prussia and Lithuania, to the Carpathians south of Przemyl, the Polish frontier to be defended included the Slovak border and formed a huge salient with a front line of some 1,250 miles — excluding the defence requirements of Danzig and the Corridor. To defend this vulnerable salient, the Polish High Command had only 45 divisions at its disposal.

When the Germans examined the Polish Army archives after their victory in 1939, they found that the French had given several warnings to their Polish opposite numbers about the dangers of the situation. One of them, prepared by General Weygand, the French Chief-of-Staff, had advised the Poles "to base [their] defences behind the line formed by the Rivers Niemen, Bobr, Narew, Vistula, and San". And Weygand went on to add: "From the operational point of view this concept is the only sound one,

for it disposes of every possibility of envelopment and places strong river barriers in the path of German armoured formations. More important, this line is only 420 miles long, instead of the 1,250-mile front from Suwałki to the Carpathian passes."

As early as the German reoccupation of the Rhineland, Gamelin had given Rydz-Smigly the same advice during a visit to Warsaw, and he reiterated the point in his discussions with General Kasprzycki on May 16. The Polish High Command, however, replied to these French suggestions by pointing out that Poland could not continue to fight a prolonged war if she gave up the industrial regions of Upper Silesia and Łód, and the rich agricultural regions of Kutno, Kielce, and Pozna without firing a shot. For this reason General Kutrzeba, according to the German examination of the Polish archives, proposed to include these regions in the defensive perimeter, but without stationing troops further west than the Warta river or cramming garrison forces into the Danzig Corridor, which would have meant that in the north the Polish troops were stationed where they had to face a two-front war, from German Pomerania and from East Prussia.

Whatever the reasons behind it, this was a rash plan. But when Rydz-Smigly stationed a full fifth of his resources around Pozna and in the Corridor itself it smacked of megalomania — and he did this despite the fact that his Intelligence department had provided him with extremely accurate figures for the forces massing against Poland. Moreover, general mobilisation was not proclaimed in Poland until 1100 hours on August 31, and this meant that on the first day of the German attack the Polish front was held by only 17 infantry divisions, three infantry

The tragedy of this Sudeten woman, unable to conceal her misery as she dutifully salutes the triumphant Hitler, is the tragedy of the silent millions who have been `won over' to Hitlerism by the `everlasting use' of ruthless force.

brigades, and six cavalry brigades. Thirteen Polish divisions mobilised by the time of the German attack were still moving to their concentration areas, while another nine divisions were still mustering in barracks.

To crown everything, the Polish High Command was fatally vulnerable in its communications with the forces in the field. There was no adequate command structure between Rydz-Smigly and his eight army commanders, and the communication network on which he depended for control in battle was cut to ribbons by the Luftwaffe's precision attacks within the first few days of the campaign.

Blitzkrieg unleashed

This unbelievable combination of mistakes contributed greatly to the Wehrmacht's success, but nothing can detract from the thoroughness of the German preparation. Brauchitsch's plan of concentration for "Case White" was based on sound concepts of strategy, and had been explained clearly to the lower command levels. Ground and air missions were co-ordinated; every man knew what he had to do; and the result got the most out of the new concept of co-operation between an armoured army and a modern air force. Drawn up at the beginning of July, the O.K.H. Directive stated: "The objective of the operation is the destruction of the Polish armed forces. The political conduct of the war demands that it be fought with crushing, surprise blows to achieve rapid success.

"Intention of the Army High Command: to disrupt, by a rapid invasion of Polish territory, the mobilisation and concentration of

German soldiers in Poland.

the Polish Army, and to destroy the bulk of troops stationed to the west of the Vistula–Narew line by converging attacks from Silesia, Pomerania, and East Prussia."

The armoured and motorised divisions with which Germany attacked Poland totalled 55 divisions, including reserves, on "Y-Day", but by September 18 this figure had risen to 63. The front line divisions were divided into two large army groups with the following strengths and objectives:

1. East Prussia and Pomerania — Army Group North (Colonel-General Fedor von Bock).

Left flank: 3rd Army (General Georg von Kuchler), with eight infantry divisions, was to assist in the destruction of the Polish forces in the Corridor and drive south towards the Vistula and Warsaw.

Right flank: 4th Army (General Günther Hans von Kluge), with six infantry divisions, two motorised divisions, and one Panzer division, was to attack from Pomerania and destroy the main body of Polish troops defending the Corridor, cutting off the Pozna - Kutno group from the north.

2. Silesia and Slovakia — Army Group South (Colonel-General Gerd von Rundstedt).

Left flank: 8th Army (General Johannes Blaskowitz), with four infantry divisions and the S.S. motorised regiment Leibstandarte Adolf Hitler, was to

German troops parade through Warsaw, Poland.

engage the Polish forces in the Pozna-Kutno region and keep them from counter-attacking the central army of the group.

Centre: 10th Army (General Walter von Reichenau), with six infantry divisions, two motorised divisions, three light divisions, and two Panzer divisions, was to drive north-east, straight for Wielufn, Łód, and Warsaw.

Right flank: 14th Army (General Sigmund Wilhelm List), with one mountain division, six infantry divisions, one light division, two Panzer divisions, and the S.S. motorised regiment Germania, was

to strike across the Carpathians from Slovakia and pin down the Polish forces around Kraków and Przemy l.

Hitler, however, intervened and altered Army Group North's schedule. By switching its forces east of Warsaw, he made sure that any Polish forces which managed to cross the Vistula would be cut off to the east of the Capital.

For General Guderian, however, the opening of the German offensive started with near disaster. He was in command of XIX Panzer Corps and, a sound armour tactician, was well up with his forward troops. "The corps crossed the frontier simultaneously at 0445 hours on September 1," he later recalled. "There was a thick ground mist at first which prevented the Luftwaffe from giving us any support. I drove forward with the 3rd Panzer Brigade in the first wave [until it came into action]. Contrary to my orders, the 3rd Panzer Brigade's heavy artillery felt itself compelled to fire into the mist. The first shell landed 50 yards in front of my command vehicle, the second 50 yards behind. I was sure that the next one would be a direct hit and ordered my driver to turn about and drive off. The unaccustomed noise had made him nervous, however, and he drove flat-out straight into a ditch. The front axle of the half-track was bent so that the steering mechanism was put out of action. This marked the end of my drive…"

No Help from the Allies

Hitler gambled that the Western powers would not go to war for Poland and hoped to repeat his Munich success. This time he was wrong. Polish general mobilisation, however, had only been proclaimed at 1100 hours the day before the German invasion and therefore the Germans had the advantage. Moreover, due to the privations of the 1930s depression, much Polish weaponry was obsolescent. The French Army in the field totalled 30 infantry divisions, 14 of which were in North Africa, nine on the Alpine front, seven on the Western front as well as a few battalions of Pyrenean chasseurs on the Spanish frontier. This shortage of available manpower was compounded by the slow rate of mobilisation and by a defensive mentality which made early offensive adventures against Germany difficult to achieve. On September 7, the French 2nd Army Group conducted an offensive between the Rhine and the Moselle, Operation "Saar", which proved to be a fiasco.

The Blitzkrieg triumphant

The first stage of the campaign saw the Polish cavalry of the "Pomorze Army" (Pomeranian Army), under General Bortnowski, charge the tanks of Guderian's XIX Panzer Corps as they thrust across the Corridor towards the Vistula, which they crossed at Chelmno on September 6, making contact with 3rd Army on the far bank. As late as September 15–18, when the campaign was already lost, the Polish "Sosnkowski Group" (11th and 38th Divisions), marching by night and fighting by day, managed three times to break through the ring which the German 14th Army was trying to close behind it. Fighting their way across the San river, the Sosnkowski divisions managed to capture 20 guns and 180 vehicles from 14th Army.

All this was achieved under non-stop bombing raids by the Luftwaffe. Although the Polish Air Force managed to keep up sporadic air attack up to September 17, the Luftwaffe dominated the air. Luftflotten (Air Fleets) I and IV, commanded by Generals Albert Kesselring and Alexander Löhr, concentrated their attacks on communication centres, pockets of resistance, and Polish forces on the move. Luftflotte I operated with Bock's Army Group North, Luftflotte IV with Rundstedt's Army Group South. Between them, the two air fleets totalled 897 bombers and 219 Stukas.

The advantage of unchallenged air power helped the German 10th Army to win rapid successes in its advance on Warsaw. It is true that on September 8 its 4th Panzer Division failed in its attempt to take Warsaw by surprise, but two days later 10th Army reached the Vistula at Góra Kalwaria and tore the Polish "Łód

Polish civilians dig trenches.

Army" to shreds. At the same time the Polish "Prussian Army" had also been cut off, broken up, and destroyed in a battle against heavy odds. Marshal Rydz-Smigly's order for the Polish armies to withdraw eastwards had gone out on September 6, but it was already too late.

This withdrawal led to one of the most dramatic episodes in the Polish campaign. Falling back on Warsaw, the "Pomorze" and "Pozna" Armies were challenged by the German 8th Army, coming up from Łód, which tried to bar their retreat. The result was the hard-fought "Battle of the Bzura", which began on September 10. The Polish troops succeeded in capturing bridgeheads across the Bzura river near Łowicz, and drove back the German 30th Infantry Division. Thanks to Hitler's order to switch the advance east of Warsaw, Army Group North was unable to intervene fast enough to cover the flank of Army Group South. But Rundstedt rose to the crisis. While Stukas attacked the Bzura bridgeheads, the motorised and Panzer divisions of 10th Army wheeled north and caught the Polish forces in flank. There was vicious fighting around Łowicz and Sochaczew before the Poles pulled back; but at last, completely cut off and hemmed in about Kutno, General Bortnowski was forced to order the surrender of his 170,000 men on September 19.

While 8th Army closed the inner pincers of the German advance by investing Warsaw and Modlin, the plan imposed by Hitler aimed at a wider sweep to trap the remaining Polish fragments retreating east of the Vistula. This was achieved by a deep Panzer penetration led by Guderian. His XIX Panzer Corps had been transferred across East Prussia after its initial successes

in the Corridor, and on September 9 it forced the Narew river upstream of Lomza. Six days later it had driven as far south as Brest Litovsk, and its 3rd Panzer Division, pressing south towards Wlodawa, had made contact with advance units of 10th and 14th Armies from Army Group South. 14th Army, which had advanced eastwards as far as L'vov, had swung north-east to complete this link-up.

Until this time the Soviet Union had observed the letter of the Soviet–Polish Non-Aggression Pact of 1932, which, renewed on May 5, 1934, was intended to run until the end of 1945. But when it became obvious that the destruction of the Polish Army was imminent, Moscow decided to intervene in order to make sure of the territories (east of the line formed by the Narew, Vistula, and San rivers) conceded to the Soviet Union by the secret protocol attached to the German–Soviet Non-Aggression Pact. At 0300 hours on September 17, Vladimir Potemkin, Deputy Commissar for Foreign Affairs, told Polish Ambassador Grzybowski that "the fact is that the Polish State and its Government have ceased to exist".

"For this reason," ran the note which Potemkin read to Grzybowski, "the treaties concluded between the Soviet Union and Poland have lost their validity. Abandoned to its own fate and deprived of its rulers, Poland has become an area in which could develop all manner of circumstances potentially dangerous to the Soviet Union. This is why, having maintained its neutrality up to now, the Soviet Union cannot remain neutral in the present situation.

"The Soviet Union can no longer remain indifferent to the

sufferings of its blood-brothers the Ukrainians and Belorussians, who, inhabitants of Polish territory, are being abandoned to their fate and left defenceless. In consideration of this situation the Soviet Government has ordered the High Command of the Red Army to send its troops across the frontier and to take under their protection the lives and welfare of the populations of the western Ukraine and western Belorussia." The note had been drawn up with the full agreement of Germany, which had undertaken not to conclude an armistice with Poland.

The Polish Ambassador refused to accept this note, but a few hours later large Red Army forces crossed the frontier and pushed motorised and armoured columns westward towards Vilna, Brest-Litovsk, Kovel', and L'vov. Within days their spearheads had made contact with Wehrmacht troops in Galicia and along the River Bug.

The intervention of the Red Army ended the last vain hopes of the Polish High Command for prolonging resistance in a last-ditch campaign in eastern Galicia with their backs to the Rumanian frontier. On the morning of September 18, President Mocicki, Colonel Beck, and the remainder of the Polish Government, together with Marshal Rydz-Smigly, fled to Rumania and claimed political asylum. Poland's formal resistance was over.

Poland: erased from the map of Europe

During this 18-day campaign the German armies had largely over-run the demarcation line agreed between Stalin and Ribbentrop on August 23. This led to a new settlement between Moscow and Berlin: the "German-Soviet Treaty of Delimitation and Friendship", signed on September 28 by Ribbentrop after another journey to Moscow. The agreement, which split Poland in two, was made at Stalin's insistence, as he refused to countenance a German suggestion for the establishment of a Polish state of 15 million inhabitants.

In this partition agreement, Germany accepted the inclusion of Lithuania into the Soviet sphere of influence; in compensation, the parts of the province of Warsaw already conceded in the agreement of August 23, plus the entire province of Lublin, were conceded to Germany. In central Poland the new demarcation line connected the Vistula and Bug rivers; in Galicia it remained on the San river, for Stalin refused to give up the petroleum wells of Drohobycz and Boryslaw.

Another protocol declared that the Soviet Union would not make any difficulties for citizens of Estonia, Latvia, and Lithuania who might wish to leave the Soviet zone of influence, taking their personal goods with them. In this agreement, Stalin and Hitler renewed the anti-Polish engagements which had bound together the Romanovs and Hohenzollerns in Imperial days. "The undersigned plenipotentiaries, on concluding the German-Soviet Treaty of Delimitation and Friendship, have declared their agreement on the following points:

"The two parties will tolerate in their territories no Polish agitation affecting the territory of the other party. They will suppress in their territories all beginnings of such agitation and inform each other concerning suitable measures for this purpose.

The same day, September 28, Warsaw surrendered after 14

Warsaw in flames after Stuka attack.

days of heroic resistance. Luftwaffe bombing had set the city flourmills ablaze, and the filtration and pumping stations for the water supply had been more than half destroyed. A humane commander, General Blaskowitz of the German 8th Army allowed the honours of war to Warsaw's defenders, who had been galvanised by their leader, General Rommel, formerly the commander of the "Łód Army". Among the prisoners-of-war was General Kutrzeba, who had broken out of the Kutno pocket with four divisions. Modlin capitulated a few hours before Warsaw.

The last shots of the campaign were fired in the Półwysep Hel peninsula, north of Danzig, where Admiral Unruh surrendered with 4,500 men on October 2.

When Hitler broadcast to the German people on September 30, he announced the number of Polish prisoners taken as 694,000, compared with German losses of 10,572 killed, 3,400 missing, presumed dead, and 30,322 wounded.

"On October 5," General von Manstein recalled, "a big military parade was held, which unfortunately ended with a disagreeable incident showing Hitler's bizarre attitude towards his generals. A table had been laid at which Hitler and his generals could sample some soup prepared by the field kitchens. But when he saw the white tablecloth and the flower decorations which had been provided in his honour, Hitler turned brusquely aside, tasted two or three mouthfuls of soup, chatted briefly with the soldiers, and got straight into his aeroplane. Apparently he wanted to show his close ties with the people. But I doubt that this gesture was really to the taste of our brave grenadiers, who would have understood perfectly that if the Head of State chose to eat with his

German soldier fastens Swastika to obelisk erected on the line of the polar circle.

generals he would be paying equal homage to the troops."

For its part, the Red Army rounded up some 217,000 prisoners, many of whom were destined to die in Russia in circumstances that will be examined in due course. About 100,000 Poles managed to escape to the West via Rumania and carry on the fight against Germany from France and Britain.

All quiet on the Western Front...

On September 13, General Georges, commanding the French North-East Front, taking Poland's defeat as virtually completed, ordered General Prételat "not to advance beyond the objectives attained, but to strengthen your dispositions in depth and to arrange as soon as possible for replacement divisions to relieve your front-line divisions, in particular the motorised divisions".

So ended Operation "Saar", which had cost the French Army 27 killed, 22 wounded, and 28 missing. General Vuillemin's air force had lost nine fighters and 18 reconnaissance aircraft. Both Gamelin and Georges later justified this decision to halt operations against Germany on the following grounds. Everything suggested that with Poland annihilated, Hitler would turn against the West with his full strength, with the assurance of a superiority of about 100 divisions to 60. Moreover, it was possible that Mussolini, drawn by the ease with which Poland had been conquered, might attack France himself before the Alpine passes were snowed up and rendered impassable.

German Navy Ship disembarks troops in Norwegian invasion

German soldiers remove Polish street signs.

Soviet Foreign Commissar Vyacheslav Molotov signs the German-Soviet nonaggression pact; Joachim von Ribbentrop and Josef Stalin stand behind him.

Baloon from the baloon barrage squadron at the Tower of London.

As was natural, the civilian population of Great Britain had certain preconceived ideas about the nature of the war to which they were committing themselves on September 3, 1939. These ideas were derived from a multitude of sources — experience in World War I, books, newspaper accounts of events such as the bombing of Guernica in the Spanish Civil War, and realistic, convincing films like "The Shape of Things to Come". Thus the people of Britain expected their declaration of war to unleash the hordes of German bombers waiting to raze London to the ground.

Nor were the civilians the only ones to predict an immense aerial bombardment: so too did the prophets and advocates of strategic air power in the armed forces.

But the British steeled themselves in vain. The bombers did not come. They were not to do so until the later stages of the Battle of Britain, for no nation in the world possessed a bomber fleet capable of dealing a decisive blow against a target such as London in a single night.

So the opening of hostilities was an anti-climax. Instead of cataclysmic and shattering total war there was only the crushing of Poland and then nothing, no action at all on the Western Front or over the embattled nations of Europe.

An American Senator, William Borah, dubbed it the "Phoney War". Chamberlain called it the "twilight war". To the Germans it was merely the "Sitzkrieg", the "sitting war".

The German generals who were the architects of the defeat of France. Manstein, the Chief-of-Staff of Army Group "A", and Rundstedt, his commander, felt that the "right hook" plan for the invasion of France, as used in World War I, was not the right one to produce decisive results. Manstein was of the opinion that Army Group "A" should be made the main striking force, and that the German offensive should consist of a "left hook" through Sedan and up to the Channel coast.

Western Front: the Rival Plans

France and Great Britain rejected the "arrangement" for the partition of Poland proposed to Western powers by Hitler in a speech to the Reichstag on October 5.

Fall Gelb (Case Yellow): the original aim was to push through to gain Dunkirk and Boulogne as the basis of an offensive against England. Lt-Gen. Erich von Manstein called for the complete destruction of all enemy forces in the field. This views were largely shared by Hitler, who called for concentration on Army Group A in the south, which was to advance through the Ardennes and secure a bridgehead across the Meuse at Sedan.

The Dyle Plan: this was the Allied defensive position in Belgium which superseded the "Escaut" Plan, which had involved a longer front. In the Dyle Plan the 9th Army would advance to a line Mezieres-Namur with its units deployed west of the Meuse; the 1st Army would take up a position between Namur and Wavre, and the B.E.F. would hold the line between Wavre and Louvain, where it would establish contact with the Belgian Army. Giraud's 7th Army would be held in reserve west of Antwerp.

Pocket Battleship Graf Spee in flames.

The Graf Spee lies scuttled having been destroyed by her own crew rather than fall into enemy hands.

Battle of the River Plate

The German navy posed a considerable threat to Britain's maritime trade with its 11-inch pocket battleships, of which Deutschland (North Atlantic) and Admiral Graf Spee (South Atlantic and Indian Ocean) were in operation at the outbreak of war. After a feint into the Indian Ocean, Admiral Graf Spee, which was due back in Germany for running repairs, came upon the British Force "G" under the command of Commodore Harwood, comprising the heavy cruiser Exeter and the two light cruisers Achilles and Ajax. The British force was split in the hope of dividing the enemy fire, though in the event Captain Hans Langsdorf chose to concentrate his fire on the Exeter, which was forced to retire. Harwood's force disengaged and Langsdorf retreated into Montevideo harbour to lick his wounds. With a 72-hour time limit imposed by the Uruguayan authorities and reports of heavier British reinforcements, Langsdorf eventually scuttled his ship in neutral waters.

Finland: the Winter War

After the German-Soviet Treaty of September 28, 1939, the Soviet Government imposed "mutual defense agreements" upon Estonia, Latvia and Lithuania which they then wished to extend to Finland. On October 14, a Finnish delegate in Mosow listened to a number of requests by the Soviets, including the ceding of islands in the Gulf of Finland and the withdrawal of the frontier in Karelian Isthmus between the Baltic and the Lake Ladoga. There was deadlock in the discussions and on November 30 the Soviets invaded Finland with an estimated 19 rifle (infantry) divisions and five tank brigades. Marshal Carl Gustav Mannerheim, C-in-C of Finland's armed forces, had nine divisions at his disposal. This meant that 120,000 Finnish troops faced 300,000 Soviet troops who were supported by 800 aircraft. The Finns, however, were well equipped to operate in the terrain which gave them ample cover, while Soviet divisions were bogged down in impassable forests and lakelands. By the end of 1939 the Red Army had suffered a series of resounding and humiliating defeats. The Soviets lost about 27,500 dead against 2,700 Finnish dead and wounded.

The Soviets came back on February 1, 1940 with an estimated 45 divisions and an overall superiority of three to one over the Finns. Despite further heavy losses, the Soviets broke through Mannerheim's line on February 11, forcing him to retreat. The Finns sued for peace and on March 12 the Russo-Finnish Treaty was signed in Moscow by which Finland was to cede Viipuri district, lease Hango Peninsula, cede Salle district, cede her portion of Pybachiy Peninsula in Lapland and build a railway between Murmansk and Kemijarn.

There was support for Finland among the Allies, and Churchill, among others, saw the strategic advantage of cutting off the iron-ore supplies to Germany. Although the British and French put together an expeditionary force to land at Narvik on March 13, 1940, Sweden and Norway refused to allow them in. The Allied plan to mine the leads and land troops at Narvik was delayed by inter-Allied disagreements, allowing the Germans to take the initiative.

In Britain, the people had a chance to prepare themselves for the bombing offensive, which though it had not come when first expected, was nevertheless thought to be inevitable. Air raid precautions were improved, prefabricated air raid shelters mushroomed in the gardens of the major cities, shop windows were taped in a dazzling variety of patterns to prevent them from shattering as a result of bomb blast, and most noticeable of all, the black-out was enforced stringently. In shops, offices, and private homes the windows had to be screened so that not a chink of light showed from the outside; many people constructed rigid screens to bolt on to the window-frame, which considerably simplified the nightly ritual of "putting up the blackout". Those who were careless or late risked the humiliating experience of a warden's stentorian voice roaring, for the whole street to hear, the words which quickly became a catch phrase: "Put that light out!" Nocturnal pedestrians were urged to wear white, men were told that they would be safer if they let their shirt-tails hang out, but accidents on the roads reached proportions so alarming that the government was forced to sanction dim street lighting to reduce

The defeated Finnish defenders of Kuhmo return home after the signing of the Finnish-Soviet peace accord.

them.

The novelty of such measures soon wore off, however. Within a few weeks it was estimated that at least a third of the boxes. in which people were meant to carry their gas masks wherever they went were in fact being used to carry sandwiches, cosmetics, and the like.

All the while, children were evacuated from the major cities and sent to stay with families in safer areas, mostly the rural parts of the West Country. At the same time, able bodied girls were asked to volunteer for the Land Army, an organisation which it was hoped would free large numbers of men for war work by providing women to take their places on the farms.

The two most important measures, however, were the increase in conscription and the introduction of rationing. There was a list of reserved occupations, persons on which were exempted from conscription, but the exigencies of the war meant that the list had to be abridged considerably by the end of the year. Food rationing was introduced in early November. Each citizen was issued with a Ration Book containing a number of coupons for such items as sugar, bacon and butter, which the shopkeeper removed or marked each time a purchase was made. A large number of other foods were added to the list of rationed goods from time to time throughout the war. But all this was only the thin end of the wedge. May 10, 1940 was to alter it all.

The Fate of Neutral Norway

The German Navy under Grand-Admiral Raeder were acutely aware of the strategic importance of Norwegian ports for U-Boat and surface raider operations. After the British stopped the German supply ship Altmark and liberated British prisoners in Norwegian territorial waters, Hitler issued two directives on February 26 and March 1, which stated that Norway must be dealt with before the Western Front offensive was launched. This would include the invasion of Denmark. The operation was named Weserubung and consisted of two army corps, an air force corps and every serviceable warship in the fleet. The attack went in on April 8, amidst Norwegian vacillation, and

House in Aandalsnes, Norway burning after a German bombing attack.

Narvik soon surrendered. Sola airfield and Stavenger were taken by German paratroops. In Denmark, King Christian X yielded to Hitler's ultimatum. The British Home Fleet under Admiral Forbes, consisting of two battleships, one battle cruiser and 21 destroyers, sailed from Scapa Flow on April 7 with the Admiralty prevaricating as to his real objective. Eventually Forbes was ordered to intercept the Scharnhorst and Gneisenau, taking him away from the main action on the Norwegian coast. Despite having lost the initiative, the British hit back heroically with an attack by the 2nd Destroyer Flotilla and Captain B.A.W. Warburton-Lee up the Vestfjord leading to Narvik. Warburton-Lee was killed but his force sank two German destroyers, damaged three others and went on to sink the vital German ammunition supply ship Rauenfels.

Badly equipped British troops proved to be no match for a well-balanced German force which made the most of its available resources and which was ably supported by the Luftwaffe in the form of X Fliegerkorps. On May 28, Narvik was taken by the 13th Foreign Legion Demi-Brigade reinforced by the Norwegian 6th Division but the Allies abandoned the campaign at the start of Fall Gelb in France and Narvik was left to fall back into German hands.

Chamberlain's Government fell in the face of the clear lack of support shown by its own members.

Norwegian troops hand over rifles to German soldiers

General Erich von Manstein discussing invasion plans with his officers.

As we already know, the plan which was evolving painfully in Hitler's mind for the attack on France through the Low Countries had already been given an almost definitive form by General Erich von Manstein, Rundstedt's Chief-of-Staff at Army Group "A" H.Q. in Koblenz.

On January 12, with the offensive once again imminent, Manstein sent another memorandum to O.K.H., again with Rundstedt's approval. In this document he restated his doubts about the results which could be gained by the current plan, repeating his former arguments, but this time giving suggestions which he believed would result in the total destruction of the enemy.

Taking account of all that was known of the enemy strength and dispositions, Manstein argued that at best the current O.K.H. plan could only result in sterile and bloody trench warfare from the Somme estuary to the Maginot Line. This meant that the November 20 directive, which aimed at bringing Army Group "A" to the Meuse at Sedan, could only be considered an inadequate palliative. Manstein believed that the revised attack would only make sense if driven home on the left bank of the river. As he saw it, these were the objectives which should be given to Army Group "A":

"While one army on the south of the front acts as a flank guard to the whole operation by taking up an approximate position on the line Carignan-Thionville, it is essential that another army, having crossed the Meuse at Sedan, drives to the south-west. This attack will defeat any attempt by the enemy to re-establish himself between the Aisne and the Oise by counter-attacking. Throwing the enemy south of the Aisne might even prevent him from forming a continuous front on the line Thionville-Stenay-Aisne-Somme. This second attack would also assist the redeployment of the northern wing [Army Group "B"] towards the south.

"A third army, forcing the line of the Meuse between Dinant and Fumay, will drive towards Saint Quentin to take in flank the enemy forces retreating to the Somme before the advance of the northern wing. Even if this fails, it will clear the way to the Somme for the northern wing.

"Only the execution of this plan will result in a decisive victory over the French Army."

The transfer of the centre of gravity of the attack to the Meuse between Dinant and Sedan implied that Rundstedt's army group should be reinforced with more armoured units and an additional army; but O.K.H. did not reply to Manstein's memorandum of January 12 and refused to forward it to O.K.W. However, the question was soon raised again as a result of two war games. One

of these was held at Koblenz on February 7; the other was held on the 14th at Mainz, the H.Q. of General List's 12th Army, with Halder present.

Given the known enemy strength in the Ardennes sector, the war game showed that Guderian's XIX Corps could reach the Meuse at Sedan on the fourth day of the attack. What should then be done? Cross the Meuse on the fifth day, was Guderian's opinion. "Absurd," noted Halder in his diary for February 7. O.K.H. would not be able to decide in which direction the offensive should be strengthened until the third day of the attack, which meant that a methodical attack could not be launched across the Meuse until the ninth or even the tenth day.

Several days before, however, Colonel Rudolf Schmundt, who had succeeded Hossbach as Hitler's aide, had been told by the Führer to make an inspection of the front.

On his way to Koblenz on January 30, Schmundt had occasion to hear of the objections which Manstein had been raising about the O.K.H. plan. Manstein's arguments impressed him so much that when he returned to Berlin his principal colleague, Captain Engel, noted: "Schmundt was very excited and told me that he had heard Manstein propose a plan identical to the one which the Filhrer was constantly proposing to us, but in a much more sophisticated form." Although there is no record of Schmundt's report to Hitler, there is no doubt that he passed on Manstein's idea to Hitler and that the latter received it with delight, as a specialist opinion which justified the prompting of his "intuition".

But this was the last personal inter vention made by Manstein. On February 8 he left Koblenz to take command of the XXXVIII

Corps, which was being formed at Stettin. To Manstein, this was "indubitable" proof that O.K.H. wanted to "rid themselves of an interloper" who had dared to oppose one of its plans. In Panzer Leader, Guderian echoes this opinion. But in fact this transfer — which carried promotion with it — had already been envisaged as far back as the preceding autumn; and it was Halder who, on February 26, put Manstein's name at the head of the list of suitable candidates to command the "armoured wedge" on which victory or defeat would depend.

On February 17, after a dinner which he had given in honour of the newly-appointed corps commanders, Hitler led Manstein into his office and invited him to speak freely about what he thought of the coming offensive. Manstein recalled that "with astonishing speed he grasped the points of view which the army group had been defending for months. He gave my ideas his full approval."

Hitler backs Manstein

Hitler accepted Manstein's plan so completely that on the following day he summoned Brauchitsch and Halder and gave them a summary of what he had heard on the previous evening, omitting nothing but Manstein's name. "One fine day," wrote General von Lossberg, "during a conference at the Chancellery, Brauchitsch and Halder were surprised to see Hitler take a pencil and draw on the map the axis of advance suggested by Manstein in his project to drive towards Abbeville and the sea; and they heard Hitler declare that this direction looked very promising for the main effort! And everyone was astonished by Hitler's strategic

brilliance — but it was the justification of Manstein's idea."

Preparation for Defeat

In 1940 the French Army was insufficiently equipped for a defensive war, with a small number of mines and anti-tank weapons. French military doctrine during the inter-war years relied on the ideal of the "directed battle", carefully regulated by high command. The French High Command also showed little interest in the potential of modern technology like the tank. The French air force was poorly developed and incapable of giving French armour the necessary air cover.

On the German side, the Reichswehr carefully studied many of the successes and failures of German tactics in the First World War and Lt.-Col. Heinz Guderian, a disciple of Captain B.H. Liddell Hart, conducted extensive tactical training with dummy tanks. Guderian recommended that the armour should be organised in large mechanised units of all arms in order to overcome the hiatus between armour penetration and infantry support. Guderian had the support of Hitler in the creation of the Panzer divisions, which amounted to six when Germany went to war in 1934. Four more were formed soon after, along with four motorised infantry divisions of SS troops. This amounted to 17 divisions organised into three corps. They could depend on the close co-operation of the lethally accurate Ju 87 Stuka dive-bomber as well as an effective anti-aircraft arm.

Brauchitsch and Halder raised no objections to the change of plan thus L thrust upon them. They themselves had arrived at similar conclusions. In fact, the manoeuvre which O.K.W.

Junkers JU87 dive bombing French positions.

had just accepted had been strongly recommended by Colonel Heusinger of the O.K.H. Operations Staff for several weeks. Heusinger, in turn, had been encouraging his colleague Schmundt to press for the plan's acceptance.

Events now moved quickly. On February 24 Brauchitsch put his signature to the new version of the Fall Gelb concentration plan. Kluge's 4th Army was now transferred from Army Group "B" to Army Group "A", which would also receive Weichs' 2nd Army, once the Meuse had been crossed. The armour was

reorganised as Panzergruppe Kleist — the armoured wedge or battering ram which was to punch through the Allied front in the Charleville-Sedan area and drive towards the Somme estuary. Panzergruppe Kleist contained the following units:

(a) *XIX Panzer Corps (Guderian)* — 1st, 2nd, and 10th Panzer Divisions;

(b) *XLI Panzer Corps (Reinhardt)* — 6th and 8th Panzer Divisions;

(c) *XIV Motorised Corps (Wietersheim)* — 2nd, 13th, and 29th Motorised Divisions.

In addition there were the 5th and 7th Panzer Divisions

German artillery units crossing the river Maas, Belgium.

attached to 4th Army, which now came under Rundstedt's command. As a result, Army Group "A" now totalled 45½ divisions — seven of them Panzer divisions and three of them motorised. Bock, whose Army Group "B" had contained 42 divisions according to the original directive of October 29, was reduced to 29 divisions, and he protested against this severe weakening of his command. Would his two remaining armies be strong enough to carry out their missions — 6th Army to force the Albert Canal, keystone of the Belgian defences, and 18th Army's key mission, to conquer Holland?

Guderian speaks his mind

O.K.H. rejected the complaints from Army Group "B". However, not all the army commanders shared in the optimism which Guderian and Manstein had managed to instil into Halder and Brauchitsch. Guderian's memoirs contain a significant passage which reveals this.

On March 15 "a conference took place attended by the army and army group commanders of Army Group 'A', accompanied by General von Kleist and myself, in the Reich Chancellery. Hitler was there. Each of us generals outlined what his task was and how he intended to carry it out. I was the last to speak. My task was as follows: on the day ordered I would cross the Luxembourg frontier, drive through southern Belgium towards Sedan, cross

Gun turrets on the Maginot Line, France.

the Meuse and establish a bridgehead on the far side so that the infantry corps following behind could get across. I explained briefly that my corps would advance through Luxembourg and south Belgium in three columns; I reckoned on reaching the Belgian frontier posts in the first day and I hoped to break through them on that same day; on the second day I would advance as far as Neufchâteau; on the third day I would reach Bouillon and cross the Semois; on the fourth day I would arrive at the Meuse; on the fifth day I would cross it. By the evening of the fifth day I hoped to have established a bridgehead on the far bank.

"Hitler asked: 'And then what are you going to do?' He was the first person who had thought to ask me this vital question.

I replied: 'Unless I receive orders to the contrary, I intend on the next day to continue my advance westwards. The supreme leadership must decide whether my objective is to be Amiens or Paris. In my opinion the correct course is to drive past Amiens to the English Channel.' Hitler nodded and said nothing more. Only General Busch, who commanded the 16th Army on my left, cried out: 'Well, I don't think you'll cross the river in the first place!' Hitler, the tension visible in his face, looked at me to see what I would reply. I said: 'There's no need for you to do so, in any case!'

"Hitler made no comment."

The German airborne assault on the Low Countries was launched at dawn on May 10. It was aimed at the key sectors of the Dutch front, at the Albert Canal bridges, and at Fort Eben Emael, and its effect was not limited to significant strategic advantages for Bock's Army Group "B". Because of their sensational nature, these airborne attacks helped to prolong Allied illusions as to where the main weight of the German offensive really lay, though they also achieved important results themselves.

The attack was made by 7th Airborne Division (Student), a Luftwaffe unit, and by 22nd Infantry Division (Sponeck), an army airborne division, with troops and equipment suited to their varying missions. They had the all-important air support of Kesselring's Luftflotte II.

The 22nd Division had to take The Hague and if possible obtain the submission and co-operation of the Dutch Crown. As he was expecting to have to request an audience from Queen Wilhelmina, the divisional commander, General Graf von Sponeck, set out in full-dress uniform. The division's plan was to take the airfields at Valkenburg, Ypenburg, and Ockenburg — lying to the north, east, and south of The Hague respectively — and close in on the capital from there. But the Dutch I Corps, facing the North Sea, had been alerted in time. A furious battle ensued, in which 22nd Division lost the airfields which had been surprised by the paratroops; Sponeck himself was wounded, and by late evening about 1,000 German prisoners were being shipped off to England from the North Sea port of IJmuiden.

The 7th Airborne Division, however, had much better luck. Its troops occupied part of Rotterdam and Waalhaven airport and held their positions in the face of Dutch counter-attacks, thanks to the close support of the aircraft of Luftflotte II. At Dordrecht the Germans held both banks of the Maas, although some troops had been dropped in the wrong places. Above all they had taken the Moerdijk bridges across the Maas estuary and so prevented their destruction. The 7th Airborne Division had therefore cleared a corridor which gave the German 18th Army access to the heart of the Dutch Vesting Holland. But would 18th Army be able to get to Moerdijk before the spearheads of the French 7th Army?

A House Divided

The Allies' Dyle Plan depended upon two major conditions if it was to succeed: sufficient advance warning of the German offensive and that General Giraud's 7th Army should not be committed prematurely on the extreme left of the Allied line. On March 20 it was decided to go ahead with a variant of the Dyle Plan, which involved the 7th Army moving into the line between the Schelde at Antwerp and the Maas, in order to cover the perceived extra threat to Holland. Dutch dispositions called for a readjustment of Belgian dispositions in order to close a gap between Hasselt and Weert, something which the Belgians rejected. The Belgians also refused to allow Allied armies into Belgium before the German attack actually began and provided little information about their plans and defences. Overall the French reserves were poorly disciplined, unready and susceptible to anti-British Communist propaganda.

German Paratroopers landing on Rotterdam.

Opposing Forces May 10, 1940

German   136 divisions available, including 10 armoured and seven motorised, for the Western offensive out of 157 in total.

3,634 from line aircraft of all types, 1,562 bombers and 1,016 fighters.

Allies   135 divisions (nine Dutch, 22 Belgian, 10 British and 94 French). Belgian Air Force: 50 relatively modern fighters, including Hurricanes. French Air Force: 418 Morane-Saulnier and 406 Curtiss Hawk fighters plus some bombers.

Royal Air Force: 130 fighters and 160 bombers as well as 60 reconnaissance aircraft.

At dawn on May 10 the Dutch post guarding the bridge at Gennep spotted a patrol of Dutch-uniformed soldiers escorting a handful of German deserters. When the little column reached the bridge it opened fire on the Dutch guards and captured it. The men were all members of the Brandenburg Detachment, specially trained for this sort of mission. Similar attempts were made at Nijmegen and Roermond, but they failed. However, the success at Gennep opened the road to 's Hertogenbosch for the German 18th Army headed by 9th Panzer Division.

Dutch resistance was uneven. It was tougher on the Grebbe Line (defended by the II and IV Corps) than on the Peel Line, where the III Corps, as mentioned above, had only been intended to slow down the German advance before falling back. The corps' withdrawal, although an orderly one, left the 1st Light Mechanised Division, the vanguard of Giraud's French 7th Army, exposed. Giraud's position had deteriorated even more by the evening of May 11, for the Belgian Army on his right flank was abandoning the Albert Canal and preparing to withdraw to the Antwerp-Louvain line. And by the evening of May 12 the 9th Panzer Division had made contact with the troops of the 7th Airborne Division holding the Moerdijk bridges.

By May 13 the situation along the Dutch front had become so grave that Queen Wilhelmina and her Government had resigned themselves to leaving the country. An appeal to Britain for help had produced no results, and could not have done. France, too, had been asked for help. But it would have been impossible for Giraud to have sent his 60th and 68th Divisions into Zeeland. The Belgian retreat meant that he dare not push his left flank forward to Moerdijk and Dordrecht. In any case, his movements were hampered by the Stuka attacks of VIII Fliegerkorps.

German Paratrooper jumping from a Junkers JU52/3M.

German Paratroopers landing largly unopposed.

Rotterdam blitzed; Holland surrenders

On the afternoon of May 14 the notorious "horror raid" on Rotterdam took place. The bombers came at the moment when the Dutch and Germans were parleying for the surrender of the city, and General Rudolf Schmidt, commanding XXXIX Panzer Corps, was not able to make contact with the aircraft of Luftflotte II and call off the attack.

Some 25,000 houses were razed, rendering 78,000 homeless. But instead of the figure of 35,000 killed which was announced at the time, today the Dutch claim only 900, and this is the figure which should be accepted.

Considering the situation of the Dutch troops who had been forced back from the Grebbe Line, and determined to spare Utrecht from Rotterdam's fate, General Winkelman made the decision to surrender. His army had lost 2,100 killed and 2,700 wounded. He signed the instrument of capitulation at 0930 hours on May 15, only surrendering the forces under his direct orders, which excepted Zeeland. But Queen Wilhelmina and the Dutch Government continued the struggle in exile, giving the Western Allies the benefit of the Dutch colonies and their resources, a merchant fleet of nearly three million tons, and the well-trained and battleworthy warships of the Dutch fleet.

At the time when General Winkelman ordered the cease-fire, the Belgian Army was preparing to give battle without further retreat, having fallen back to the sector of the Dyle Line agreed in the earlier discussions between King Léopold and Gamelin. It is true that the Belgian resistance along the Albert Canal had lasted barely 48 hours instead of the four or five days hoped for by the

German troops cautiously move forward.

Belgian Government and the Allied High Command; but there was no connection between the surprise attacks which had forced this early withdrawal and the disaster on the Meuse on May 15.

The epic of Eben Emael

At dawn on May 10 the three regiments of the Belgian 7th Division were holding the line of the Albert Canal with their right flank anchored by the fortified complex of Eben Emael, which was armed with two 120-mm guns and 16 75-mm guns in armoured turrets and casemates. While General van Overstraeten was worried about possible sabotage of the demolition planned for the canal bridges, the Bélgian dispositions seemed to be reassuring.

But no account had been taken of the imaginative flair of Adolf Hitler, who had taken a personal interest in the planning for surprise capture of the Albert Canal bridges, despite the scepticism of O.K.W.

The key factor in this daring enterprise was to be the glider. Paratroops would not have been able to land directly on their objectives with the same precision, and in any case the time needed to re-deploy them would have given the Belgian defenders plenty of warning. For these reasons a special detachment of 42 gliders had been formed under the command of Captain Walter Koch, made up of 424 men (including pilots). For months, the Koch Detachment had undergone rigorous training under conditions of the strictest secrecy — training which included the

German troops advance in Holland.

specialised use of explosives.

On the left bank of the canal, the gliders of the Koch Detachment landed right in the middle of the defences covering the bridges at Veldwezelt and Vroenhoven. Profiting from the confusion caused by the appearance of these unfamiliar aircraft, which had seemed to the Belgians to be ordinary types in difficulties, the Germans cut the cables to the bridge demolition charges as well as the telephone lines, and then threw the explosive charges into the canal. At Canne, however, where the terrain prevented such an accurate landing, the Belgians had time to blow up the bridge, and then inflict heavy losses on the Germans. Meanwhile, 11 gliders had landed on top of Fort Eben Emael.

Seventy-eight assault pioneers, equipped with two and a half tons of explosives, set about the turrets and casemates of the fort, according to the plans which had been worked, out in great detail and rehearsed a hundred times during the previous months. Unlike the Maginot Line, Eben Emael was not protected by outer works-and within minutes many of its strong-points had been neutralised by explosive charges thrust into the gun-slits or by hollow-charge blocks applied to their armour.

Deployed along a front of 11¼ miles, the Belgian 7th Division was unable to launch any prompt counter-attacks against the bridgeheads won by the Koch Detachment at Vroenhoven and Veldwezelt. The least activity on the part of the Belgians provoked pitiless Stuka attacks. The Belgians fought back as best they could, but they could not prevent the Germans from bringing in reinforcements as planned. In the morning, machine gun sections were parachuted in; and about noon the advance units of 4th Panzer Divisions made contact. The latter had found the Maastricht bridges destroyed and had crossed the Maas as best they could.

At 0530 hours on May 11 the German pioneers opened a first 16-ton bridge to their traffic, which accelerated the arrival of 4th Panzer Division and XVI Panzer Corps, the spearhead of the German 6th Army (Reichenau). Towards noon, rendered helpless by neutralisation of its guns, the garrison of Fort Eben Emael surrendered to the 51st Pioneer Battalion under Lieutenant-Colonel Mikosch; and by the evening the Belgian 7th Division was out of the battle. These events caused King Léopold to issue the withdrawal order already 'mentioned. The Allies launched repeated air strikes against the Albert Canal bridges, the destruction of which would have cut off the bulk of Reichenau's advance units. But the fighters and anti-aircraft batteries of the Luftwaffe guarded their charges well. On May 11–12, 39 Belgian, French, and British bombers attacked the bridges. Of these, 17 were shot down and 11 were damaged beyond repair — and the Allied bombs caused virtually no damage at all.

The Belgian retreat caused a certain number of incidents of which the most unpleasant centered around the defence of Louvain — a disagreement between the commander of the Belgian 10th Division and Major-General B. L. Montgomery, commanding the British 3rd Division.

The Allies get under way

Despite all this, the withdrawal had been completed by the evening of the 13th; and King Léopold issued the following stirring order of the day: "Our position improves day by day; our ranks are tightening. In the decisive days which lie ahead do not spare yourselves; suffer every sacrifice to halt the invasion. As on the Yser in 1914, the French and British troops are relying on us; the safety and honour of the country demand it."

At 0630 hours on May 10, Captain Beaufre, adjutant to General Doumenc at G.H.Q. Land Forces, Mantry, reported to Gamelin at Vincennes. The latter was about to set in motion the complicated Dyle-Breda manoeuvre, swinging the 1st Army Group into the Low Countries — a plan which would involve five armies, 13 corps, 41 divisions: a total of about 600,000 men. Beaufre found Gamelin in an optimistic mood, "pacing up and down the corridors of the barracks, humming audibly with a martial air…"

The day before, however, Paul Reynaud had been trying to obtain Gamelin's dismissal in a session of the French Cabinet. Failing because of the opposition of Daladier and his Radical Socialist colleagues, Reynaud had offered his resignation to President Lebrun, but withdrew it when the news of the German offensive broke. Gamelin, although under the shadow of imminent disgrace, faced the new crisis with confidence.

He held to his *War Plan 1940* of February 26, in which he had described how the Allied armies would respond to any German invasion of the Low Countries. "They [the Allies] will be well placed to go over to the counter-offensive, for the enemy will be venturing into open terrain. Only the battlefield of Luxembourg, Belgium, and southern Holland lends itself to a decisive battle in the country outside the fortified systems and lines of obstacles. If the Germans gain possession of the Albert-Meuse line upstream of Liège, a counteroffensive can be made by turning the Albert Canal from the north and by a thrust between the Ardennes and the Moselle, which would turn the Meuse."

Gamelin was obviously much less defensively-minded than is usually believed. But his projected "thrust between the Ardennes and the Moselle" — a spectre which was indeed to keep Hitler awake at nights — was a pipe-dream. To make it a reality, Gamelin would have had to have at his disposal on May 10 a standing reserve-and this did not exist and was not even being formed.

"There he [Gamelin] was," de Gaulle recalled, "in a setting which recalled a convent, attended by a few officers, working and meditating without mixing in day-to-day duties … In his *Thébaïde* [ivory tower] at Vincennes, General Gamelin gave me the impression of a savant, testing the chemical reactions of his strategy in a laboratory."

But even more serious was the multi channelled chain of command. Gamelin's Vincennes H.Q. had no radio transmitter. Georges, Commander-in-Chief of the North-East Front, was 40 miles away from Vincennes at la Ferté-sous-Jouarre, while yet another key command area was Doumenc's G.H.Q. Land Forces, 22 miles from Vincennes at Mantry.

Another snag was that the French army commanders were far from unanimous in their attitude towards Gamelin's plan. When

the bad news of the events on the Albert Canal came in on May 11, General René Prioux, whose cavalry corps had the task of covering the arrival of 1st Army in its new sector at Gembloux, told his army commander, General Blanchard that: "because of the weak Belgian resistance and the enemy superiority in the air, the Dyle manoeuvre seems difficult and it would be better to settle for the Escaut manoeuvre."

Blanchard agreed. He passed the message to his army group commander, Billotte, who telephoned Georges a few minutes later: "General Blanchard is pressing for the Escaut solution. I am leaving for 1st Army and will go on to General Prioux to see to the completion of the Dyle manoeuvre, which must be carried out."

In this difference of opinion the impetuous Billotte was in the right. The DyleBreda manoeuvre in course of execution could not have been adjusted to fit the Escaut solution, and in any case the rendezvous arranged with the Belgians had to be kept. As for the danger from the air, it was in fact less serious than Generals Prioux and Blanchard imagined — but for reasons which, if those generals had known them, would only have added to their worries. For to give the Ardennes venture its best chance of success, it suited Hitler not to impede the FrancoBritish advance into the Low Countries.

First blood to the Allies

Although the Belgian retreat to the Antwerp-Louvain line was justified, it had been made earlier than envisaged, which meant that during the Allied advance into Belgium the brunt fell upon

The German Rifle Section of a motorised infantry unit, during their invasion of Flanders, May 1940.

General Prioux's cavalry corps for a few days.

The corps consisted of the 2nd and 3rd Light Mechanised Divisions, commanded respectively by Generals Langlois and Bougrain. On the 13th the cavalry corps came to grips with XVI Panzer Corps in the region of Merdorp, on the Liège-Namur road. German historians claim that the armoured units of 3rd Light Mechanised Division, mainly engaged with 4th Panzer Division, showed inferior manoeuvrability; furthermore, Major-General Stever's orders were transmitted more efficiently than those of General Bougrain.

But by the morning of the 15th the French 1st Army, thanks to the delaying actions fought by the cavalry corps, was in position between Namur and Wavre with six divisions in the line and one in reserve. Here it underwent the assault of the German

Lieutenant Witzig, leader of the assault troops who captured fortress Eban Emel, and was awarded the Knights Cross for his work.

6th Army, driven home with heavy Stuka attacks. At Gembloux, where Bock had hoped to drive in the French line with the tanks of XVI Panzer Corps, the Germans were held and indeed repulsed by the French IV Corps under General Aymes. At 1630 hours Reichenau called off his troops, planning to resume his advance with a more orthodox, set-piece attack.

Meanwhile, Reichenau's XI Corps had tried to rush Louvain, but the German troops were promptly flung out by a timely counter-attack by the British 3rd Division under General Montgomery. All in all, north of Namur the Allies had the best of May 15. But to the south, at Sedan, matters were altogether different, causing Gort and Blanchard to issue orders for a retreat on the evening of the 15th.

The success of the Dyle manoeuvre depended on the firm holding of the Allied centre by the French 2nd and 9th Armies which, to the west of Longuyon and the south of Namur, blocked the exits from the Ardennes and held the line of the Meuse. All Huntziger's 2nd Army had to do was to hold the positions which it had occupied since September 1939; from Sedan to Givet the same applied to Corap's 9th Army, but his left and centre had to advance from the Rocroi-Fourmies region and take up defensive positions along the Belgian Meuse between Givet and Namur.

A crucial question: had General Billotte been given too much responsibility for one man to carry, dynamic though he was? In the Dyle-Breda manoeuvre he had naturally been more deeply concerned in the intricate manoeuvres of his 7th and 1st Armies than in the static sector of his front (9th and 2nd Armies). And to crown everything, a conference with Daladier, King Léopold, and Gort's Chief-of-Staff, Lieutenant-General H. R. Pownall, at Casteau near Mons on May 12, had charged Billotte with co-ordinating the activities of all Allied armies on Belgian territory. This meant that he had to direct six armies-seven, in fact, if a successful link-up with the Dutch could be achieved. To sum up, Billotte alone was the man who would have to handle the attacks made by the armies of Bock and Rundstedt.

Everything points to the fact that the French troops holding the central "hinge" of the Allied front should have been put under a tighter command, which would have kept them better in hand and compensated for many of their deficiencies.

Without exception, the troops holding the "hinge" were not only mediocre or worse, but also badly equipped and deployed on much too long a front. Facing the onslaught of Army Group "A" between Namur and Sedan were seven French divisions spread out along a sector of 85 miles. The current doctrines of defensive warfare demanded at least 12. Moreover, on May 13 only one out of these seven divisions was an active unit: the 5th Motorised Infantry Division on Corap's left flank. The rest were all reserve divisions, as were the 55th and 71st Infantry Divisions of 2nd Army, defending the Sedan sector.

These reserve divisions were appallingly short of anti-tank and anti-aircraft guns. The 55th and 71st Divisions had between them only 21 out of the 104 25-mm anti-tank guns which they should have had, and the 102nd and 61st Divisions of 9th Army were even worse off. As a result of the paucity of the anti-aircraft defences in the Sedan sector, the Stukas could operate virtually without opposition: 9th Army had only three groups of 75-mm and three batteries of 25-mm A.A. guns, despite the requests of General Corap, who required three times this number.

The ground defences had been neglected during the severe winter and had suffered even more from insufficient supplies of concrete and steel obstacles. In certain sectors of the French Meuse, sandbags had taken the place of proper obstacles. Anti-tank mines, which could have made up for many of these deficiencies, had only been supplied in pitifully small numbers. On the Belgian Meuse, fortifications were virtually non-existent.

The Ardennes drama

On the morning of May 10, Corap and Huntziger sent their cavalry divisions across the Franco-Belgian frontier into the Ardennes, to act as a screen while 9th Army took up its new positions. The 1st and 4th Light Cavalry Divisions, plus the 3rd Brigade of Spahis from 9th Army, managed to reach the Ourthe, but the 2nd and 5th Light Cavalry Divisions from 2nd Army engaged numerous German tanks near Arlon and fell back.

On the 11th, several cavalry engagements confirmed that the Germans were making a major effort in the Ardennes region. The 2nd and 5th Light Cavalry Divisions were thrown back with heavy losses and Corap was obliged to withdraw his cavalry to the left bank of the Meuse. The impression gained from these first skirmishes was confirmed by air observation: "The enemy seems to be preparing an energetic thrust in the direction of Givet," concluded General d'Astier de la Vigerie, commander-in-chief of the air forces attached to 1st Army Group, in his bulletin at noon on May 11.

Advancing against the four French light cavalry divisions and two cavalry brigades with their 300 tanks and armoured cars were no less than seven Panzer divisions totalling 2,270 armoured vehicles. Given these odds it is hardly surprising that the French cavalry units failed to sustain their delaying action for more than 48 hours, instead of the envisaged four days. But they retreated in good order and blew both bridges across the Meuse after they crossed in the afternoon of May 12.

On the evening of the same day, Major-General Erwin Rommel's 7th Panzer Division reached Houx lock, on the Meuse downstream of Dinant. Urged on by Rommel's enthusiasm, the 7th Motorcycle Battalion crossed the weir to the left bank and profited from a small gap between the French 5th Motorised Division and the 18th Division to infiltrate, scale the bank, and establish a provisional bridgehead. General Bouffet, commanding the II Corps in Corap's army, was well aware of this weakness in his front, but the battalion which he had sent that afternoon to cover the weir at Houx had completely failed to carry out its orders.

Rommel's tiny pocket on the left bank should have been pinched out on the following morning; but under Stuka bombardment the French infantry failed to co-ordinate with the tanks of the 4th Light Cavalry Division which headed the French counter-attack, and by the evening of the 13th the enterprising Rommel had gained enough ground for his sappers to begin bridging operations across the river.

It will be remembered that 7th Panzer Division, together with the 5th Panzer Division (Hartlieb) following in its tracks, formed Hoth's XV Panzer Corps, which in turn belonged to Kluge's 4th Army. During the night of May 12–13, the French in the sector of 102nd Division observed a heavy column of enemy traffic heading for Monthermé, slightly downstream of the junction of the Meuse and Semois rivers. "It's an onrush, all lit up," reported a French airman-for the Germans, seeing the weakness in the Allied flank, were speeding forwards with all lights on.

Breakthrough at Sedan

The 6th and 8th Panzer Divisions (Kempff and Kuntzen), of Reinhardt's XLI Panzer Corps, formed the right-hand column of Kleist's Panzergruppe. They attacked at 1600 hours on May 13, only to meet furious resistance from the machine gunners of the 42nd Colonial Demi-Brigade. But all the courage of the latter was no substitute for anti-tank guns. The Pzkw IV tanks and self-propelled guns of the Panzer divisions took up position along the right bank of the Meuse and systematically blasted the French machine gun nests on the opposite bank.

When the latter had been silenced a German battalion crossed the Meuse on inflatable rafts and after bloody fighting took the little town of Monthermé. But they could get no further because of sustained resistance and awkward terrain. This setback at Monthermé was, however, largely eclipsed by the total victory of Guderian and his XIX Panzer Corps in the Sedan sector.

On hearing the alarming reports from the cavalry units, Huntziger had committed his reserve-71st Division-to assist X Corps. On the morning of the 13th the 71st closed up on the right wing of the 55th Division on the Meuse. Yet the forces released by this move had not reached to their new sector when the Stukas of VIII Fliegerkorps launched a series of intensive attacks, pinning down the French troops where they stood.

On May 10 the XIX Panzer Corps — 1st Panzer Division in the lead, 2nd Panzer Division on the right, and 10th Panzer Division on the left — had surged forward at dawn. While crossing the BelgianLuxembourg frontier some time was lost because of determined resistance from the Chasseurs Ardennais of Keyaerts Group and by extensive road demolitions. But by the evening of the 11th Guderian's leading Panzers had broken through to the Semois, having covered 60 miles in 48 hours. Considering the delay suffered by 2nd Panzer Division, Guderian had wanted to postpone a further advance from the 13th to the 14th, but Kleist, wanting to be sure of a close co-ordination between his two corps, would not agree. On the 12th, Guderian closed up his divisions and agreed with Luftflotte III (General Hugo Sperrle) on the measures to be taken to ensure close co-operation between the Luftwaffe and the ground troops.

From noon to 1600 hours the Stukas intensified their attacks, meeting no opposition at all. They concentrated on the artillery positions of 55th Division, while eight concentrations of 10.5-cm and 15-cm guns were pounding a front of 2,700 yards to speed the crossing of Kirchner's 1st Panzer Division. The French emplacements on the left bank of the Meuse were knocked out one by one by high velocity 8.8-cm A.A. guns.

About 1600 hours, when the French guns covering the Meuse had been silenced, the S.S. Motorised Regiment Grossdeutschland, sent to help 1st Panzer Division, was ferried to the left bank in assault boats with outboard engines and on inflatable rafts, and was flung straight into the fray. The resistance of the French 55th Division fluctuated. Some units fought until the Germans broke into their positions; others gave up at the first shot. On the whole, however, the badly-trained reservists who made up the division broke and fled before the German infantry. Worse still, about 1800 hours at Bulson, five miles from Sedan, before any German tanks had crossed the Meuse, panic spread to a French regiment of heavy artillery and to the rear areas like a forest fire. Guns were blown up, telephone lines cut, and terrified troops took to their heels.

Guderian recalled the crossing in the following words: "I was now anxious to take part in the assault across the Meuse by the riflemen. The actual ferrying must be nearly over by now, so I went to St. Menges and from there to Floing, which was the proposed crossing-place of 1st Panzer Division. I went over in the first assault boat. On the far bank of the river I found the efficient and brave commander of the 1st Rifle Regiment, Lieutenant-Colonel Balck, with his staff. He hailed me with the cheerful cry: 'Pleasure-boating on the Meuse is forbidden!' I had in fact coined the phrase myself during the training that we had had for this operation, since the attitude of some of the younger officers had struck me as too light-hearted. I now realised that they had judged the situation correctly."

By midnight, the German penetration south of Sedan was deep enough for Guderian's sappers to open their bridges to XIX Panzer Corps' heavy vehicles. On the right, the forward units of Veiel's 2nd Panzer Division had been halted in front of Donchery, while on the left Schaal's 10th Panzer Division had only gained a little ground around Wadelincourt on the left bank of the Meuse. But the, French 55th Division had been scattered, leaving 500 dead; the 71st Division was on the brink of destruction and the French had lost 80 guns.

The following day Guderian headed his corps for Abbeville and the Channel, swinging to the west, sending 1st and 2nd Panzer Divisions across the River Bar and the Ardennes Canal. Grossdeutschland and 10th Panzer Division guarded the flank of the German penetration around Stonne. On the 14th and even on the 15th, an energetic counter-attack across the rear of 1st and 2nd Panzer Divisions by the 3rd Armoured and 3rd Motorised Divisions of Flavigny's XXI Corps would have had a very good chance of restoring the French front along the Meuse. But nothing was done. Flavigny was content to "contain" the south flank of the pocket. Meanwhile the German flak gunners defended the Sedan bridges with a high degree of skill; 170 bombers, most of them British, were flung against the bridges in near-suicidal missions, and 85 were shot down.

So it was that the 664 tanks of 1st and 2nd Panzer Divisions carved through the right flank of the French 9th Army. Corap tried to block their path by stationing his 3rd Brigade of Spahis and his 53rd Division between the Meuse and Poix-Terron; but the Spahis immolated themselves in a heroic but desperate engagement at La Horgne and the 53rd Division, a typically down-at-heel French reserve unit, went to pieces at the first encounter.

At the same time, further to the north, 8th Panzer Division crossed the Meuse at Nouzonville, midway between Monthermé and Mézières,, shouldering aside the French 61st Division. In the sector of the French XI Corps, covering Mariembourg and Philippeville, French resistance wilted on the 14th and collapsed on the 15th, for 5th Panzer Division had followed 7th Panzer across the Meuse, and their combined 654 fighting vehicles had caught the French 22nd and 18th Divisions in the act of installing themselves along an overstretched front of over 23 miles. Neither of these two French divisions was motorised; neither of them had more than 12 battalions apiece in the line on May 12; and both had been counting on at least 48 more hours to complete their redeployment. General Doumenc of G.H.Q. Land Forces, writing of the disorganisation of 9th Army after the German crossing of the Meuse, recalled: "The battlefield retained its air of chaos until evening. These are the impressions of one staff officer: 'On the way, we passed through the swirling smoke of a fuel convoy which had been bombed and was burning beside the road. Further on, an artillery group had been attacked while still on the march. On the roadway and the verges a series of enormous shell craters and many dead horses showed that the attack must have been irresistible.'"

The fate of 1st Armoured Division only made matters worse. Billotte had put this division at the disposal of 9th Army; it had 156 tanks, of which 66 were the formidable Char B type, and prepared to counterattack towards Dinant. But it was surprised while refuelling by the tanks of XV Panzer Corps and virtually wiped out. The technical reason was simple enough: French tanks were laboriously refuelled by tankers, while the Germans used the

Tired and dirty but flushed with success, the German paratroopers who captured Eben Emael after their return to their barracks in Germany

smaller, handier "Jerricans" for the job. To crown the disastrous events of May 15, 4th North African Infantry Division, going to the help of the French XI Corps, was cut to pieces as well.

In the morning of May 16 the advance units of XIX and XLI Panzer Corps, thrusting forwards from Poix-Terron and from Monthermé, joined hands at Montcornet deep in the rear of the French XLI Corps. Further to the north the XV Panzer Corps — still subordinated to the German 4th Army — crossed the Franco-Belgian frontier near Fourmies.

In four days of battle Panzergruppe Kleist and XV Panzer Corps had destroyed eight divisions of 9th and 2nd Armies and had smashed open a breach of 81 miles in the front held by Billotte's 1st Army Group. And through that breach some 2,200 tanks and armoured cars were streaming towards the Channel. Were the French Government and High Command to blame for relying on a "defensive" front along the Dyle? That has always been the view of Paul Reynaud. But it is true to say that the defeat of this "defensive" army group had come about because it was not defensive enough. How would the story have turned out if, on May 13, the Germans had run into tough, well-prepared French troops waiting for them on the left bank of the Meuse? But to do this the French would have needed enough antitank guns to prevent the Panzers on the right bank from knocking out the French fortifications across the river, and enough anti-aircraft guns to breakup the precision attacks of the deadly Stukas.

German assault gun STUG III. During the French invasion.

At 0300 hours on May 14, Captain Beaufre accompanied General Doumenc to G.H.Q. "North-East" for a conference with General Georges. With an emotion which 25 years had not dispelled, Beaufre recalled what took place.

"The atmosphere is that of a family keeping vigil over a dead member. Georges rises briskly and comes up to Doumenc. He is terribly pale: 'Our front has been pushed in at Sedan! There have been some failures …' He falls into an armchair and a sob stifles him. It was the first man that I had seen weep in this battle. I was to see many others, alas! It made a dreadful impression on me.

"Doumenc, surprised by this greeting, reacts at once. 'General, this is war, and this sort of thing always happens in war!' Then Georges, pale as ever, explains: two second rate divisions have fallen back after a terrible bombing attack. The X Corps has signalled that its position has been overrun and that German tanks arrived in Bulson around midnight. Another sob. All the others in the room stand there, struck silent.

"'Come, General,' says Doumenc, 'all wars have seen collapses like this! Let's look at the map. We'll see what can be done!' He speaks strongly in this encouraging vein and it does me good to hear it.

"Standing before the map, Doumenc sketches a manoeuvre: the gap must be closed, 'plugged' as they used to say in 1918."

Chaos on the roads

Doumenc's optimism was praiseworthy, but he was unaware of two elements of the situation which would ruin his hopes. Nor could he foresee the development of a third element, which would prove equally disastrous.

To start with, during the "collapses" of 1914 and 1918, neither Moltke nor Ludendorff had adequate means with which to keep up the pace of the German pursuit; large cavalry units were far too vulnerable, their endurance was poor, and no cavalry unit had as much fire-power as the infantry anyway. Second, neither Joffre in 1914 nor Pétain and Foch in 1918 had to worry about heavy enemy air attacks in their rear areas, which in 1940 wrought havoc among the troop columns and supply convoys, and the key road and railway junctions.

The third element which Doumenc had not foreseen was the flooding chaos of the refugee "exodus". Jean Vidalenc, who has made a special study of the phenomenon, has estimated that by August 13, 1940, some two and a half million refugees had reached the south, centre, and south-west of France. And this figure does not include the refugees who had found their way home after a brief flight, or who had made for Mayenne or Brittany. The same panic in Belgium also caused bottleneck jams on the roads, and badly disrupted the military operations of May–June 1940.

The whole grim story demonstrates the total failure of French propaganda, which had been entrusted to Jean Giraudoux at the beginning of hostilities. His concept of "psychological warfare" ended by making five million Frenchmen take to their heels.

The overall phenomenon of the civilian exodus put incredible problems in the way of the Allied conduct of military operations, and must be ranked with the other reasons for the Allied defeat. As Vidalenc puts it:

"Columns of refugees now struggled along the roads … In the grey light before the dawn, shadows appeared like pale ghosts, their features drawn by their march through the night, through the day before, perhaps through the day before that; the poor went on foot, pushing before them barrows laden with odds and ends. Their feet were raw with blisters; some would stop by the road-side and ease off their shoes. Horse-drawn vehicles, cars piled high with mattresses, suitcases, parcels tied with string, lashed together with straps or held by elastic cords, passed by the tramping pedestrians, their owners wearing the clothes selected as most useful or most valuable when the time came to leave home. The most harrowing sight was the children … It was frightful to hear their terrified young voices screaming: 'The planes, mummy, the planes!' and to know that they must already have seen death falling from the skies…"

"We have been defeated…"

At 0400 hours on May 15 Billotte tele phoned Georges and made it clear that 9th Army was "on the brink of catastrophe". Billotte suggested that Giraud, a real leader of men, should take over; he would be able to create the "psychological shock" capable of stiffening 9th Army. Corap, as yet reproached with nothing, should take over 7th Army. By about 1600 hours Giraud, forcing his way along roads choked with refugees, had reached the H.Q. of 9th Army at Vervins-but he brought with him nothing but a solitary aide-de-camp, while he would have liked to hurl the motorised units of his former army against the flank of the Panzer breakthrough.

At 0730 on the 15th Winston Churchill had been jerked

from his sleep by the news that Paul Reynaud was calling him by telephone. Churchill picked up the receiver and received Reynaud's message: "We have been defeated … the front is broken near Sedan; they are pouring through in great numbers with tanks and armoured cars." In his memoirs Churchill admits that he was unable to recall the precise words used by his French colleague. But he is clear enough about his own reply in which, like General Doumenc, he pointed to historical precedent:

"All experience shows the offensive will come to an end after a while. I remember the 21st of March, 1918. After five or six days they have to halt for supplies, and the opportunity for counter-attack is presented. I learned all this at the time from the lips of Marshal Foch himself."

There was equal astonishment at the French Ministry of National Defence. William Bullitt, the American Ambassador, was in the same room as Daladier when Gamelin telephoned with the news of the breakthrough at Sedan and the Panzer advance. Bullitt was so impressed by what he heard that on the 16th he did not hesitate to cable Washington: "It seems clear that without a miracle like the Battle of the Marne, the French Army will be completely crushed."

This is how Bullitt recalls the scene: "But the telephone rang from Vincennes; the Supreme Commander was calling the Minister. Suddenly Daladier shouted: 'No! That's not possible! You are mistaken!'

"Gamelin had told him that an armoured column had smashed through everything in its path and was at large between Rethel and Laon. Daladier was panting. He found the strength to shout: 'You must attack!' 'Attack? With what?' replied Gamelin. 'I have no more reserves.'

"Daladier's features crumpled more and more. He seemed to be shrinking as I watched.

"The grim conversation ended with the following exchange:

"'So this means the destruction of the French Army??' 'es, this means the destruction of the French Army!'"

Bullitt added that there was already a certain amount of dissension between the French and the British. The latter considered the French attitude "defeatist"; and the analysis of Bullitt's despatch made by the American historian William L. Langer held that the British were showing reluctance to "risk their own fortunes in the common cause".

Churchill orders in more British reinforcements

None of this was in Churchill's mind when he arrived in Paris on the afternoon of May 16 for a meeting with Reynaud, Daladier, and Gamelin at the Quai d'Orsay. Within five minutes Churchill had been put in the picture and convinced of the gravity of the situation. "I then asked," says Churchill in The Second World War, 'Where is the strategic reserve?' and breaking into French, which I used indifferently (in every sense): 'Où est la masse de manoeuvre?' General Gamelin turned to me and, with a shake of the head and a shrug, said 'Aucune.' " Churchill did not know that in Gamelin's "Breda" variant the Supreme Commander had ignored the repeated advice of his subordinates and, for political rather than for strategic reasons, had committed Giraud's 7th Army, which should have formed the "masse de manoeuvre".

French anti-aircraft gun.

But this disastrous news did not prevent Churchill from agreeing to send ten more fighter squadrons to join Air-Marshal A. Barratt's force in France, which had already suffered considerable losses.

While these discussions were being held, the archives of the French ForeignOffice were being burned by panic-stricken officials in the gardens of the Quai d'Orsay. But as evening drew on the tension eased. Near Rethel, a German colonel strayed into the French lines. He was captured, badly wounded, and was found to be carrying a map on which Arras and Abbeville were marked as the objectives for the Panzer forces, which had been expected to appear before Paris on the following day.

The breach widens

When the first reports of the disaster at Sedan came in, General Georges did what he could to restore coXitinuity to the Allied front. On the eve of the German crossing of the Meuse he had ordered four divisions to head for the threatened sector. The following day, to ease the strain on Billotte, Georges took 2nd Army under his direct orders and diverted General Touchon's 6th Army, originally intended to cover the Swiss frontier, to the Aisne. On May 17 General Frère — not Corap — was given command of 7th Army and ordered to re-establish contact with 9th Army in the region of St. Quentin.

Thus between May 12–17 some 20 divisions were given new orders which would head them towards the breach in the Allied

British troops waiting by the roadside in France.

line-a redeployment which necessitated the smooth running of over 500 trains and 30,000 vehicles. But the plan was ruined from the outset by Luftwaffe attacks. During the same period, May 12–17, German bombers cut the French railway network in hundreds of places, isolating the sector exposed to the offensive of Panzergruppe Kleist.

This disruption caused a general delay of 24–36 hours before the first troops intended for the sectors of 6th and 7th Armies arrived on the scene. Some units were delayed by constant bombing, while others were forced to set out prematurely. The tracked vehicles of 2nd Armoured Division became pinned down on a stretch of railway 75 miles long between Tergnier and Hirson; the wheeled vehicles of the division, struggling along the roads, became separated from the tanks; and so 2nd Armoured Division was scattered into a shower of small, unto-ordinated detachments, and could not play its part in Georges's "plugging".

Up at the front the Germans made good use of the chaos in

the Allied camp. As night fell on May 16, 7th Panzer Division forced the Franco-Belgian frontier near Solre-le-Château. Any commander other than Rommel would have been satisfied with this success, but he drove on through the darkness, surprised Avesnes at midnight, dashed past Landrecies, and arrived before Le Cateau at dawn on the 17th after a breath-taking advance of over 30 miles. He had scattered the surviving units of 18th Division and 1st Armoured Division, sweeping in thousands of prisoners, whom the Germans barely had time to disarm in their haste. Above everything else, Rommel had thrown the rear areas of 9th Army into inextricable confusion.

In his G.H.Q. at Münstereifel, however, Hitler did not share the optimism of his front-line commanders. Halder argued in vain that the Allies were not strong enough to launch a counter-attack towards Sedan, and that the Panzers could be allowed to thrust forwards without any unreasonable risk. Hitler remained paralysed with anxiety, and at noon on the 17th, after a visit to O.K.W. with Brauchitsch, Halder noted: "Apparently little mutual understanding. The Führer insists that he sees the main danger coming from the south. (In fact, I don't see any danger at all!) Therefore, infantry divisions must be brought up as quickly as possible to protect the southern flank; the armour will have to rely on its own resources to enlarge the breakthrough to the north-west."

And a few hours later the same subject arose after an intervention from O.K.W. by telephone: "2100 hours. A rather disagreeable day. The Führer is terribly nervous. Frightened by his own success, he fears to take risks and would prefer to curb our initiative. Reasons for this: his fears for the left flank. Keitel's telephone calls to the army groups and the Führer's personal visit to Army Group 'B' have produced nothing but trouble and doubt." Next morning, the same problem …

This friction between O.K.W. and O.K.H. had its repercussions on the battlefield, resulting in order and counter-order. On the night of May 15–16 Guderian received a telephoned order from Kleist to postpone his advance until the supporting infantry had joined up. When Guderian protested vehemently he was authorised to resume the advance, but only for 48 hours. Despite a brilliant success on May 16, Guderian received a visit from Kleist on the morning of the 17th. Kleist had come to restate this unfortunate halt order to his impetuous subordinate, and he did so in terms which provoked Guderian to offer his resignation.

On Rundstedt's direct orders General List, commander of 12th Army, ended the dispute in the early afternoon. He settled it with a compromise which, made at the moment when every hour counted, saved the campaign from petering out. Guderian, restored to the command of XIX Panzer Corps, would obey Kleist's order to halt, which came from O.K.H. But he was authorised to continue with a "reconnaissance in force" towards the west. Seizing this loophole, Guderian chose to make his "reconnaissance in force" with the entire fighting strength of 1st and 2nd Panzer Divisions, pushing a first bridgehead across the Oise at Moy on the evening of the 17th. By noon on the 19th Guderian's tanks had taken Péronne.

Allied dislocation gets worse

Meanwhile, XVI Panzer Corps (Hoep ner's 3rd and 4th Panzer Divisions) had also been transferred to Rundstedt's Army Group "A" and subordinated to 4th Army. This meant that nine Panzer divisions, followed by six motorised divisions, were now operating on Billotte's right flank and driving across his rear. Billotte's withdrawal to the Escaut Line was being hampered not only by the attacks of Army Group "B" but by Luftwaffe attacks and by the disorganised flood of refugees.

In this total confusion it was hardly surprising that all reinforcements for Giraud's army were sent in vain. Rendered meaningless by the course of events, his orders had either been drawn up for units which no longer existed, or only reached formations which were not yet in their correct position. On May 16 Giraud transferred his H.Q. from Vervins to Wassigny — but the break-up of 2nd Armoured Division after the destruction of 1st Armoured meant that he no longer had enough forces with which to counterattack, while Rommel was driving towards Landrecies and Guderian's advance towards the Channel was being slowed down only by the untimely and cautious intervention of Kleist.

Giraud is captured

When Giraud decided to fall back from Wassigny to Le Catelet he found all the roads blocked before him. Abandoning his car for an armoured car, he tried in vain to get through the enemy lines-and at dawn on the 19th he himself became a prisoner of the Germans.

General Doumenc has described how it happened: "General Giraud had left Wassigny at 1600 hours, taking only two officers with him. After moving to the H.Q. of 9th Division he passed through Busigny only to find that the enemy had armoured cars at every cross-roads on the main road from Cambrai to Le Catelet. By nightfall they had got to within seven miles of Le Catelet; the little group abandoned its vehicles and after a three-hour march by the compass had reached Le Catelet, part of which was burning … they ran into a German outpost and there was an exchange of shots, after which they took refuge in a wood. The General then ordered the party to separate. He himself was slowed down by an old wound and stopped behind a hedge at the side of the Cambrai road. Then he saw, coming from the south, a column of French trucks with a gun-carrier in the lead, which had bypassed Le Catelet. He climbed into the gun-carrier and knocked out the first German tank which they encountered, only to run into three more tanks. He then threw himself into a farmhouse which seemed isolated."

"Unhappily," runs Giraud's own account, "this farmhouse was filled with refugees who probably gave us away to the first Germans who questioned them. Within minutes three German tanks surrounded the farmhouse while a large column drew up on the road. We were rapidly discovered; I thought it would be useless to risk the life of the young troops there, and I ordered them not to fire. It was 6 o'clock; we were prisoners."

At about 2000 hours on May 20, Spitta's battalion from Veiel's 2nd Panzer Division was the first German unit to reach the Channel coast near Noyelles. Meanwhile, at Péronne, Corbie,

French Char Leger H-35 light tanks.

Amiens, and Abbeville, other formations of XIX Panzer Corps had outrun the retreating French 7th Army and had established bridgeheads across the Somme.

Thus the "plugging" of the ruptured Allied front attempted by General Georges had failed completely. But did it ever have a chance of success? As Doumenc says, the breach could have been closed by a mass redeployment of the five infantry and three motorised divisions which were frittered away in vain attempts to assist 9th Army. But to have got this group of divisions into position (with its right on St. Quentin and its left on Le Cateau) by May 16 would have required it to have been set in motion on May 12, at the very moment when Rommel's motorcyclists reached the Meuse.

"This simple statement of dates," comments Doumenc, "shows the impossibility." Certainly, but there can be no denying that it was fatal to have committed 7th Army in the "Breda" variant of Gamelin's plan. If 7th Army had been retained as the mobile reserve for 1st Army Group, as Georges had originally recommended, it would probably have been a very different story. Instead, Giraud was forced, like General Soubise after the Battle of Rossbach in the old song, to go wandering about looking for his troops, lantern in hand …

Napoleon went further. He is quoted as having said: "In war, a major disaster always implies a major culprit."

Town square after bombardment by German artillery.

Thus when Gort ordered "Frankforce" to retire from Arras on the evening of the 23rd, and then, on the 25th, broke away from the manoeuvre laid down for 1st Army Group, he was not waiting on the course of events. But it was certainly a timely move. If Hitler had not intervened personally on the morning of the 24th and ordered that the Panzers were not to pass the Lens–Béthune–St. Omer–Gravelines line, it is clear that Guderian could have reached Dunkirk and Malo-les-Bains on the evening of the following day.

Hitler's celebrated "halt order" before Dunkirk has been interpreted in many ways, both by German generals and historians of the war. Some have held that Hitler wished to spare the B.E.F.

the humiliation of total surrender in order to regain the favour of the British and make them more amenable to a settlement. This is hardly credible. Others have argued that Hitler wanted to give his friend and chosen successor, Hermann Göring, the chance of showing that no troops could retreat or embark under the bombs of the Luftwaffe. This explanation, however, is even thinner. The fact is that the order which spared nine British divisions and over 110,000 French troops from captivity was sent out to the German 4th Army by telephone, after a visit by Hitler to Rundstedt's H.Q. at Charleville, at 1231 hours on May 24.

According to the war diary of Army Group "A", published by the German historian Hans Adolf Jacobsen, it would appear that Hitler made this decision after a similar suggestion had been made

A Lockheed Hudson aircraft from RAF Coastal Command approaching Dunkirk on a reconnaisance patrol.

to him by Rundstedt. It is hardly surprising that after the event Rundstedt did not claim the credit for the "halt order".

The reasons given for the "halt order" were the danger involved in committing the Panzer forces in the swampy terrain around Dunkirk and the need to conserve them for Operation "Red", the second phase of the campaign. This decision, made at the top, drew the following bitter comments from Halder on May 25:

"The day began with one of those unfortunate quarrels between Brauchitsch and the Führer, over the closing stages of the battle of encirclement. The battle plan which I suggested requires Army Group 'B', by means of a heavy frontal attack, to force the enemy into an ordered retreat, while Army Group 'A', falling upon an already shaken enemy, cuts its communications and strikes the decisive blow — a job for our tanks. Now the political command has come up with the idea of fighting the decisive battle not on Belgian soil but in northern France. To cover up this political shift, the argument is that the terrain of Flanders, crossed by many water-courses, is unsuitable for a tank battle. As a result, all tanks and motorised troops must be moved quickly to the St. Omer–Béthune line.

"This is a complete reversal of our plan. I wanted to make Army Group 'A' the hammer and Army Group B' the anvil of the operation. Now 'B' will be the hammer and 'A' the anvil. But Army Group B' is facing a solid front; its progress will be slow and its losses high. Our air force, on which all hopes are pinned, is dependent upon the weather.

"This change means a stepping-up of the tempo which will need more energy than the actual plan of operations. For all that, the battle will be won, by this method or the other…"

On the following day, May 26, Hitler cancelled his decision and gave his tanks a free hand, but the time taken to get them on the move again meant that the chance of reaching Dunkirk before the British had been missed.

When Gort made his decision to retreat, he had already found himself obliged to keep close watch on his dwindling stocks of artillery ammunition. It is therefore difficult to find fault with his decision. Post-war memoirs by Gort's subordinates of 1940, such as Alanbrooke and Montgomery, conclude that Gort's decision had only one major fault, that of expecting too much from the French.

The fact remains that the French 1st Army, fighting at the bottom of the Allied pocket, was put in a difficult position by the British withdrawal; the British would have to cover only 47 miles from Arras to Dunkirk, but 1st Army, at Valenciennes, was over 62 miles from the port. When Weygand saw that his planned joint counter-attack, which should have been launched on the 26th, was now impossible, he still hoped that the 1st Army would be able to establish itself in a beach-head at Dunkirk deep enough to save the port from German artillery fire. But by the 26th the situation had deteriorated so badly that Weygand cabled Blanchard: "We (that is to say Reynaud and myself) are fully aware of the situation. You must remain the only judge of what must be done to save what can be saved, above all the honour of the colours of which you are the guardian."

German anti-aircraft unit.

Belgian resistance fades

This was not optimistic language — but it took no account of the progressive decline of the Allied situation on the Belgian sector. The Belgian Army had been retreating from the Schelde to the Lys; when Antwerp and Brussels were surrendered on May 17 on the orders of the Belgian High Command, another segment of Belgian territory had been abandoned without a fight. Nevertheless the Belgians rallied to the call of their King, holding on valiantly along their front, which ran from the Léopold II Canal to the Lys Canal, along the line of the Lys, joining the left flank of the B.E.F. at Menin.

On May 24 the German 6th Army broke through the new position at Courtrai, revealing Reichenau's intention of driving towards Ypres and cutting off the Belgian Army from the B.E.F. The Belgians hit back as best they could; two reserve divisions had entered the line, and the fine showing of the 8th Division and the 2nd Chasseurs Ardennais Division limited the effect of the German breakthrough. On the 25th the 12th Division and the 1st Chasseurs Ardennais Division, on the Lys Canal and the Lys river respectively, launched timely and vigorous counter-attacks. But the Belgian reserves were rapidly used up, and the British refused to attack the flank of the German column thrusting towards Ypres, but continued their withdrawal to Dunkirk.

The Weygand Gambit

On May 17 General Maxime Weygand, C-in-C Middle East, was ordered back to Paris from Beirut. After journeying to Belgium to assess the position, Weygand devised a plan which he presented to Reynaud and Churchill, among others: the Belgian Army should retire to the line of the Yser and the country should be flooded; the British and French should attack towards Bapaume and Cambrai with about eight divisions; the RAF should provide maximum support; the new French army group heading towards Amiens and forming a front along the Somme should thrust north to form a junction with British forces in the region of Bapaume. Britain sanctioned the movement of ten squadrons of fighters to France. Weygand believed the Allies must re-establish a continuous front between 1st Army Group and 3rd Army Group to form a "solid barrier" to prevent the Panzer forces that had ventured to the sea breaking out to the coast. Weygand's plans were wrecked, however, by a series of delays stemming from the death of General Billotte in a car accident. There was no attack by eight Allied divisions towards Bapaume and Cambrai on the 23rd or the 24th and the French 7th Army did not cross the Somme. On May 21 the British attacked at Arras with "Frankforce", the 5th and 50th divisions and 74 tanks of 1st Army Tank Brigade. Meeting with initial success, they were finally driven back, and Panzer forces headed north and north-west to besiege Calais and Boulogne.

The Belgian surrender

On May 26 the Belgian Army was still fighting, but its right was bending under the renewed attacks by Reichenau, and its left was yielding ground before the German 18th Army advancing from the direction of Antwerp. The battle was renewed at dawn on the 27th; and at 1230 hours King Léopold informed Gort that: "The moment is rapidly approaching when our troops will no longer be able to fight. The King will be forced to capitulate to avoid a disaster." Two hours later the King gave General Champon, chief of the French Military Mission, a note which told the same story: "Belgian resistance is reaching the end of its tether. Our front is fraying like a worn-out, breaking rope."

In the centre of the front a breach, 3 to 4 miles wide, was opening in the Thielt area; on the left, the 17th Division was on the point of collapse. From above, the Stukas kept up a non-stop bombardment on the artillery positions and the emptying ammunition dumps. Behind the lines, among a population of 800,000, an equal number of refugees was wandering. At 1700 hours King Léopold overruled the advice of General van Overstraeten (who wanted to wait until the following day) and sent an envoy to the German lines to discuss the Belgian surrender. But the King did not do this without having first informed Colonels Hautcoeur and Haily of the French and British Military Missions. While waiting for the German reply, King Léopold provided for the French 60th Division which had been fighting on the left of the Belgian Army, transporting it in trucks to the Dunkirk sector to be put at the disposal of General Blanchard. In the same spirit he ordered the destruction of the Yser bridges and the blocking of the ports of Ostend and Zeebrugge.

At 2230 hours the Belgian envoy, Major-General Derousseaux, returned to the Belgian G.H.Q. with the message that Hitler was demanding unconditional surrender. The Belgian Army, having hidden or destroyed its standards and colours, ceased fire at 0400 hours on May 28. The following day the last Belgian troops surrendered and Belgium's 18-day battle came to an end. In this desperate battle against the invader, the unfortunate King Léopold had rejected the attempts of his ministers to persuade him to leave the battlefield and follow them into exile. King Léopold has been criticised for his conduct in not following the example of Queen Wilhelmina, but it is a false comparison. Under the Belgian constitution he was the Commander-in-Chief of the Belgian Army, a duty which did not apply in Queen Wilhelmina's case. While German propaganda proclaimed to the Allied troops in the Dunkirk pocket: "Your commanders have fled by aircraft. Lay down your arms!", Léopold had announced to his troops: "Whatever happens my fate will be yours." Should he have broken this promise at the very moment when he was being informed of the "defection" of certain units, their morale undermined by the plotting of Flemish agitators in the pay of Hitler?

And how could the Dunkirk evacuation have met with the success it did if the Belgian Army, deprived of the commander in which it had confidence, had laid down its arms on May 26 or 27?

The Dunkirk perimeter

One fact at least is clear, however: the Belgian surrender sealed the fate of the French 1st Army around Lille. Both flanks of the 1st Army were now laid bare, and only 25 miles separated Hoth's Panzergruppe at la Bassée from Reichenau's forces at Menin on the French left. On May 28, taking Cassel and the Monts des Flandres, the Germans closed the ring round the French IV and V Corps which were dug in around Lille, Loos, and Haubourdin. These forces put up such an heroic resistance that when they surrendered, General Waeger, commander of the German XXVIII Corps, honoured them with a guard of honour from the 25th Division. General Molinier, the French commander, was allowed to retain his staff car.

General Prioux would not abandon his brave comrades of the IV and V Corps. He hung on at his H.Q. at Steenwerck and was captured there at 1245 hours on the 29th. General de la Laurencie, however, urged his exhausted III Corps north through Poperinge and Hondschoote and saved them from captivity, in a 37-mile night march along the incredibly choked roads. On the morning of the 29th he reported to Admiral Abrial, commanding at Dunkirk, with his 12th and 32nd Divisions and part of the 1st Motorised Division. The survivors of the cavalry corps did useful flank-guard service during this harrowing retreat.

Fagalde's XVI Corps was holding the Dunkirk beach-head with the 60th and 68th Divisions; de la Laurencie's troops came as a welcome reinforcement. Unfortunately, following the strict instructions laid down by the British High Command, they had to abandon most of their heavy weapons and a good deal of ammunition before they were allowed to withdraw into the Dunkirk zone, which caused some recrimination between the Allies. On the same day, May 29, the embarkation of the B.E.F. reached an encouraging figure. On that day 47,310 British troops were evacuated, while on the 27th and 28th the total had been only 25,473. The credit for this success undoubtedly must go to Vice-Admiral Sir Bertram Ramsay, Flag Officer, Dover. Four years later, Ramsay's energy and resourcefulness would be put to far better use than handling the details of an improvised evacuation under constant air bombardment: planning the Allied invasion of France in 1944.

Operation "Dynamo"

As early as May 20, Churchill had suggested that "as a precautionary measure the Admiralty should assemble a large number of small vessels in readiness to proceed to ports and inlets on the French coast". The War Cabinet agreed, and Ramsay was given the task of putting the scheme into operation. Ramsay took over everything that could float: small passenger ferry-boats from the Channel and the Irish Sea routes; coasters, trawlers, motor yachts and *schuyts* — flat-bottomed Dutch boats which had taken refuge in England.

In all some 850 commercial boats were taken over by the Admiralty, which agreed with some reluctance (in view of the needs of the Atlantic convoys) to detach 39 destroyers as escorts. But Ramsay did not content himself with putting the precious destroyers on purely defensive duties: in the teeth of the German bombers, magnetic mines, and torpedo-boats, he did not hesitate

to send in the destroyers to embark troops from the port of Dunkirk and from the beaches of Malo-les-Bains, Bray-Dunes, and De Panne, just to the north of Dunkirk.

Operation "Dynamo", as the evacuation was called, formally went into operation at 1857 hours on May 26. Informed too late of the British intentions, the French were only able to make a comparatively feeble contribution. It was not until the 28th that Rear-Admiral Landriau was put in command of the Pas-de-Calais flotilla, which finally numbered some 300 vessels of every tonnage, including 15 destroyers and torpedo-boats, under the command of Captain Urvoy de Portzamparc.

If the British War Cabinet did take its time to inform the French of its decision to re-embark the B.E.F., Winston Churchill spared no effort to see that Operation "Dynamo" should take off as many French as possible. In his note to the Secretary of State for War on May 29, he wrote: "It is essential that the French should share in such evacuations from Dunkirk as may be possible. Nor must they be dependent only upon their own shipping resources. Arrangements must be concerted at once with the French Missions in this country, or, if necessary, with the French Government, so that no reproaches, or as few as possible, may arise…"

On May 30, 120,000 men, of which 6,000 were French, were embarked. On the 31st, when Gort received the order to hand over command of the beach-head to Lieutenant-General Alexander, first III Corps and then II Corps — about 150,000 men — had been shipped back to England, together with 15,000 Frenchmen.

Destroyed Allied vehicles on the beaches at Dunkirk.

From June 1 the defence of the Dunkirk perimeter was taken over by the French XVI Corps. But it should be noted that the British spared no effort, without regard to risk, to spare their French comrades from imprisonment. By the time that Operation "Dynamo" ended on June 4, 113,000 French troops had been shipped to England out of a total of 338,226 Allied troops. That is to say that during the last four days of the evacuation 75,000 British and 98,000 French troops were embarked — and most of them on British ships.

The "miracle of Dunkirk" was only made possible by extremely difficult manoeuvres, one of which has been recalled by

Alanbrooke:

"There was little possibility of sleep that night, as the 3rd Division were moving past and I repeatedly went out to see how they were progressing. They were travelling, as we had so frequently practised for our night moves, with lights out and each driver watching the rear of the vehicle in front of him, which had the differential painted white and lit up by a tail-lamp under the vehicle. The 3rd Division through constant practice had become most proficient at this method of movement. However, with the congestion on the roads, road-blocks outside villages, and many other blocks caused by refugees and their carts, the division was frequently brought to a standstill. The whole movement seemed unbearably slow; the hours of darkness were slipping by; should daylight arrive with the road crammed with vehicles the casualties from bombing might well have been disastrous.

"Our own guns were firing from the vicinity of Mount Kemmel, whilst German artillery was answering back, and the division was literally trundling slowly along in the darkness down a pergola of artillery fire, and within some 4,000 yards of a battle-front which had been fluctuating all day somewhat to our disadvantage. It was an eerie sight which I shall never forget. Before dawn came, the last vehicles had disappeared northwards into the darkness, and I lay down for a few hours' disturbed sleep, but kept wondering how the 3rd Division was progressing."

The resistance of the 12th Motorised Division and the 32nd and 68th Divisions was beyond praise; it lasted, contrary to all expectations, until dawn on June 4. General Janssen, commanding the 12th Motorised Division, was at the heart of the fighting and was killed by a bomb; General Fagalde, commanding XVI Corps, was taken prisoner with 40,000 men. Like Vice-Admiral Abrial, "Admiral North", and Rear-Admiral Platon, who embarked under orders at midnight on the 3rd, Fagalde had been the spirit of this battle without hope.

In the narrow sealane of the Straits of Dover, seven French destroyers and torpedo-boats and six British destroyers were sunk by Stukas and by attacks from E-boats (German motor torpedo boats), together with a quarter of the small boats involved in the operation. In the air the fighters of the R.A.F. gave the Luftwaffe a hard time, greatly helping the embarkation of their comrades on the beaches; at the cost of 106 of their own machines, they accounted for most of the 156 German aircraft shot down during this phase of the campaign.

Hitler judges his enemies

Despite the undoubted setback represent ed by the Allied evacuations from Dunkirk, Hitler had scored a crushing victory. For German losses put at 10,252 killed, 42,523 wounded, and 8,467 missing, he announced that 1,212,000 Dutch, Belgian, French, and British prisoners had been taken. In addition, his armies had captured an enormous booty: from the British Army alone, the spoils taken by the Germans amounted to 1,200 field guns, 1,250 anti-aircraft and anti-tank guns, 11,000 machine guns, and 75,000 vehicles. It is not surprising, therefore, that his letters to Mussolini were flushed with optimism; but setting aside the flamboyant boastfulness, four interesting points are to be found in the letter of May 25 in which Hitler passed judgement on his opponents:

"As for the morale of our enemies, there is this to say:

1. The Dutch. They put up a much stronger resistance than we expected. Many of their units fought very bravely. But they had neither appropriate training nor experience of war. For this reason they were usually overcome by German forces which were often numerically very inferior.

2. The Belgians. The Belgian soldier, too, has generally fought very bravely. His experience of war was considerably greater than that of the Dutch. At the beginning his tenacity was astounding. This is now decreasing visibly [written some three days before the Belgian surrender] as the Belgian soldier realises that his basic

Evacuees from Dunkirk disembark at an English port.

function is to cover the British retreat.

3. The British. The British soldier has retained the characteristics which he had in World War I. Very brave and tenacious in defence, unskilful in attack, wretchedly commanded. Weapons and equipment are of the highest order, but the overall organisation is bad.

4. The French. Very marked differences appear when it comes to assessing the military capacity of the French. Very bad units rub elbows with excellent units. In the overview, the difference in quality between the active and the reserve divisions is extraordinary. Many active divisions have fought desperately; most of the reserve divisions, however, are far less able to endure the shock which battle inflicts on the morale of troops. For the French, as with the Dutch and Belgians, there is also the fact that they know that they are fighting in vain for objectives which are not in line with their own interests. Their morale is very affected, as they say that throughout or wherever possible the British have looked after their own units and prefer to leave the critical sectors to their allies."

French 4th army 280mm Schneider Howitzer.

The disastrous course of events in Flanders had forced Weygand to abandon his plan of a joint counter-attack against the "Panzer Corridor". It was even more vital, however, that the bridgeheads won by the Germans on the left bank of the Somme should be destroyed. The outcome of the defensive battle which now had to be fought between Longuyon and Abbeville depended largely upon this.

To this end the French 7th Army and the forces under Altmayer (renamed 10th Army on May 28) were sent into action along the Somme while the retreat to Dunkirk and the evacuation were still in progress.

Upstream of Péronne, the efforts of General Toussaint's 19th Division, ably, assisted by the tanks of 2nd Armoured Division under Colonel Perré, restored the French front along the Somme. Between Péronne and Amiens the Germans were also pushed back, but there they managed to hold on to their bridgehead across the river. It was hardly surprising that these counter-attacks were only partially successful. They were made by divisions which were flung into battle one by one and which, given their small numbers, had to cover too wide a front. The reduction of the Abbeville bridgehead was entrusted to de Gaulle's 4th Armoured

Division, hastily re-formed since its raids on May 17 and 19, and reinforced with six infantry battalions. The division attacked on the afternoon of May 28. It struck at the positions held by a regiment of Lieutenant-General Blilmm's 57th Division and caused much panic, for the German 3.7-cm anti-tank guns could not pierce the heavy armour of the French tanks. But because it was not promptly exploited, de Gaulle's success was fleeting. During the night of May 28–29, Blümm's force was reinforced by two 8.8-cm flak batteries, and their guns soon demonstrated, as they had done at Arras, their devastating power against tanks.

On May 29–30, the 4th Armoured Division made limited progress but failed to clear the crest of Mont Caubert; by the third day of the battle the division had taken some 500 prisoners, but it had been reduced to a mere 34 tanks. Finally called off on June 3, the counter-attack at Abbeville had achieved little — and on the 5th, Bock's army group attacked along the entire Somme front.

Weygand's defence plan

Between the last embarkations from Dun kirk and the unleashing of Operation "Red" — the second and final phase of the Battle of France — there was a pause of little more than a single day.

Although Weygand was bombarded with a constant, bewildering stream of disastrous and disconcerting news, it must be said that he reacted with promptitude and energy throughout. Most of his decisions were sound, and above all there was the powerful, morale-boosting influence which he exerted on his subordinates. In a few days he had restored the spirit of the front-line troops to a remarkable degree. And the evidence for this can be found less on the French side than in the war diaries and memoirs of the Germans.

Weygand had shown his mettle as early as May 24, in a note laying down the measures to be taken against German armour supported by aircraft. On May 26, after his new defence plan had received the unanimous approval of the War Committee presided over by the President of the Republic, he issued the following "General Order of Operations"

"1. The battle on which the fate of the country depends will be fought without any idea of retreat from the positions which we occupy now. All commanders, from army commander to corporal, must be animated by the fierce resolve to stand and fight until death. If commanders set the example their troops will stand; and they will have the right to compel obedience if necessary.

2. To be certain of halting the enemy, constant aggressiveness is essential. If the enemy shows signs of attacking on any sector, we must reply with swift and brutal counter-methods.

If the enemy succeeds in establishing a bridgehead in our front which he can use for rushing in tanks and then moving on to an armoured attack, it is essential — no matter how insignificant the bridgehead may be — to drive the enemy back to his lines with artillery fire and air strikes, and to counter-attack. Infiltration must be countered with infiltration. If a unit believes that a neighbouring unit is wavering it must not at any cost fall back but must try to restore the situation. If this is impossible it must dig in and form a 'hedgehog' of resistance. This must apply to all units from divisional right down to company level.

3. The rear areas of the main defence line must be organised, in as great a depth as possible, into a checkerboard of centres of resistance, in particular on the main roads along which the Germans have always moved. Demolition charges must be prepared.

4. Every divisional general must be in constant touch with his colonels, the colonels with their battalion commanders, the battalion commanders with their company commanders, and the captains and lieutenants with their sections and their men. Activity-Solidarity-Resolution."

Weygand's note of May 24 had anticipated the methods prescribed by this order. In the face of the "tank-aircraft tandem" attacks of the Blitzkrieg, it amounted to an improvised defensive tactic for which the French lacked sufficient means, but which nevertheless inflicted heavy losses on the victors of this first campaign in France.

Above all, Weygand believed, the Panzers must be cut off, decimated, and annihilated on a prepared battlefield. To do this meant, as he wrote: "substituting for the idea of the line the idea of control of communications", and this must be done by quartering the terrain, establishing the artillery in strongpoints and allocating a third of the artillery for anti-tank use, and by camouflaging all positions against air and ground observation.

A combination of these measures, he thought, would prevent the German infantry from following up as close support for those of their tanks which managed to infiltrate the French positions, while the tanks themselves, cut off from the trucks bringing up their fuel and ammunition, would fall victim to the crossfire of the French infantry and artillery. At this critical moment for the attacker, the defenders could send in their infantry to mop up, or to launch more ambitious counter-attacks backed by tanks.

On June 5, 1940, the French lacked sufficient forces to man such a front, as well as the thousands of anti-personnel and anti-tank mines which it required. Apart from these fatal deficiencies, however, the type of front envisaged by Weygand was strikingly similar to the German defences which stopped the British and Americans in the Normandy *bocage* country after D-Day in 1944.

Could the plan have worked?

In his book The Battle of France, 1940 Colonel Goutard condemned Weygand's plan for being "merely a return to the classical doctrine of a continuous front". But this ignores the fact that the front envisaged by Weygand was far more flexible than previous conceptions of a static defence line, and that without an armoured reserve, any other disposition than the one prescribed by Weygand on May 26 would have laid France wide open to the onrush of the Panzers.

But when Weygand, with his forces diminished by a third, prepared to fight a defensive battle against an intact enemy, did such an armoured reserve exist? In his memoirs, de Gaulle says that it did. On June 1 he proposed the formation of two large armoured units from the 1,200 modern tanks still available for action. Supplied with infantry and artillery complements, he suggested that if the larger group were posted north of Paris and the other south of Rheims they could be used as an adequate mobile reserve. As de Gaulle put it, they would be able to strike

French Char B1-Bis heavy tank driven into a bar.

at the flank "of any one of the German mechanised corps when, having broken through our front, they would be dislocated in width and extended in depth."

In his reply to General de Gaulle, prepared in 1955, Weygand excused himself for not remembering this suggestion. But he asserted that at the time he had no more than 250 modern tanks at his disposal — not 1,200 — and this bears examination. A contemporary record gives only 86 tanks — Char B and Hotchkiss — to the 3rd Armoured Division, and 50 to the 4th Armoured. The figure for the 2nd Armoured Division on June 5 is not known, but it can hardly have been much higher than that of the other two. The 7th Light Mechanised Division was a recent formation, but even if it was at full strength it would have had only 174 tanks, of which half were Somua S-35's and half Hotchkiss H-35's. Even if the 2nd, 3rd, and 5th Light Cavalry Divisions had survived the disaster, they would have been reduced to skeleton strength.

Weygand's critics have argued that to attempt to defend both Paris and the Maginot Line could only have ended in disaster. This is a facile criticism. As far as Paris was concerned, calculations had been made to determine the effect on the French war effort of- the loss of this or that line; and it was clear at the time that having already lost the industrial regions of the north, so vital to the production of tanks, it was essential to defend the line of the Somme and the Aisne.

As for the Maginot Line, it is true that shorter defensive fronts could have been selected, but at best the advantages to be gained by abandoning the Maginot Line could only have been purely military ones. The Rhine basin would have been lost, together with the strongpoints between the Rhine and the Moselle which enabled a front of 220 miles to be defended by a mere 17 divisions, of which ten were "Series B" reserve ones.

The 3rd Army Group had been transferred from the Saône to the Somme. General Garchery had handed over the 8th Army to General Laure, and 8th Army was now attached to 2nd Army Group, with the task of coping with any German attempt to cross the Rhine between Basle and Strasbourg, or to violate neutral Swiss territory. From Sélestat to Bitche stood. Bourret's 5th Army, and then, covering the Moselle valley, Condé's 3rd Army. As Weygand had redeployed many of its units to other sectors, 4th Army's strength was reduced to General Hubert's group covering

Rommel 7th Panzer division in France.

the Saar. In view of the signs which hinted at a possible offensive by the German Army Group "C" on the Saar and across the Rhine at Neuf-Brisach, General Prételat found that his 2nd Army Group had really been reduced to a dangerous level.

Paul Reynaud was born in 1878 and was trained as a lawyer. He served on the Western Front in World War I, and became a Deputy in 1919. In the early 1930's he held ministerial posts, but then fell out of favour until 1938, when he became Minister of Justice and later of Finance. He was a staunch advocate of tank warfare and opposition to Hitler. He was appointed Prime Minister on March 21, 1940, and resigned on June 16 when he failed to persuade his Cabinet to continue the war.

Weygand had promoted Huntziger from the command of 2nd Army to that of the new 4th Army Group. The 2nd Army, taken over by General Freydenberg, covered the passes of the Argonne; to the left of 2nd Army, General Réquin's 4th Army held the line of the Aisne between Attigny and Neufchâtel. The 12 divisions of the 4th Army Group had a front of 75 miles to cover; but although the Argonne forest favoured the defenders, the rolling chalk countryside of Champagne was so well adapted to tank warfare that it had been christened the "tankodrome" in French military circles.

Finally, the 150 miles of front between Neufchâtel-sur-Aisne and Abbeville were covered by General Besson's 3rd Army Group. This was made up of three armies: General Touchon's 6th Army on the Aisne; General Frère's 7th Army blocking the approaches to Compiègne and Beauvais; and General Altmayer's 10th Army on the lower Somme. With one division per 8½ miles of front,

General Besson's army group presented a very over-stretched network of strongpoints — while the Germans had seven bridgeheads on the left bank of the Somme.

Counting the 16 infantry divisions in army group or supreme command reserve, the seven armoured, mechanised, and cavalry divisions, and the four British and Polish divisions still in France, Weygand had at his disposal a force of 71 divisions. But even to arrive at this unimpressive total he had had to draw upon the reserve armies in the Alps and North Africa, despite the increasing threat from Italy.

As a result of the disastrous opening phase of the campaign, some 25 infantry divisions had been destroyed. Thirteen out of the original 31 active infantry divisions had gone, and six out of the seven motorised divisions. Six out of the original 13 light cavalry, light mechanised, and armoured divisions which Gamelin had deployed on the morning of May 10 had also been removed from the board. Nevertheless, Weygand had managed to form three striking groups out of his surviving armoured units. On June 5, 1940, they were ready for the fight: the first, under General Pétiet, around Forges-les-Eaux, the second, under General Audet, in the Beauvais area, and the third, under General Buisson, in the Vouziers area. Weygand, therefore, cannot be accused of having failed to create an armoured reserve, albeit a sadly depleted one.

Henri Philippe Pétain was born of peasant stock in 1856 and joined the army in 1876. He had a normal career and made his name in the defence of Verdun in 1916. He was appointed C.-in-C. of the French Army after the crippling mutinies of 1917 and his humane treatment did much to raise morale. In 1918 he was subordinated to the Allied C.-in-C., Foch, but promoted to Marshal just after the war. Between the wars he served in Morocco, in the government, as Inspector-General of the Army, and as Ambassador to Spain until 1940, when he was recalled to join the government.

Reynaud's "Breton redoubt"

After Weygand's plan had been accepted by the War Committee on May 25, he had to reject an idea expressed by Reynaud in a note on the 29th; this had required him "to plan for the establishment of a national redoubt around a war port, allowing us to make use of the sealanes and above all to communicate with our allies. This national redoubt should be arranged and supplied, particularly with explosives, to make it *a veritable fortress*. It would consist of the Breton peninsula. The government would remain in the capital and would continue the war by making use of our naval and air forces in North Africa."

Attractive as this idea sounded on paper, the limited resources and the lack of time at the end of May 1940 made it an impossibility. Weygand put it in a nutshell: "The organisation of a 'veritable fortress' would need, after the construction of strongpoints along some 94 miles of front, the diverting of manpower and all kinds of war material, in particular anti-tank and anti-aircraft guns. All these resources were already insufficient to meet the needs of the defence line in process of organisation along the Somme and the Aisne; there could be no question of diverting even a small part of them; for even if it had been possible, there was not enough time."

Assistance from the Allies

How much help did France receive from her allies?

In his 2nd Army Group, General Prételat had two divisions of Polish infantry who were soon to put up a magnificent fight under the most desperate conditions. So did the British 51st Division, on the left flank of 10th Army. But the British armoured division, under Major-General R. Evans, serving in the same sector, has been described by one of its officers as "a caricature of an armoured division," not even equipped with "half its official tank strength, no field guns, insufficient antitank and anti-aircraft guns, without infantry, without air cover, deprived of most of its auxiliary services, with part of its staff in a vehicle 'armoured' with plywood…"

So much for the actual forces in the field. As far as the future of the British cooperation in the Battle of France was concerned, the picture was not good. At a meeting of the Supreme War Council on May 31, Churchill held forth with his customary resolution — but when it came down to details he became reticent and vague. According to the minutes of the meeting, "Mr. Winston Churchill observed that the problem of the invasion of England had changed in appearance, and that yet again he could promise nothing before he knew what could be saved from the North.

"As far as air reinforcements were concerned, he did not have the authorisation of his Government to grant more than had been given."

When Reynaud tried to explain the "vital character of the battle of the Somme to Churchill, he received the following

25th Panzer regiment resting prior to attack on the Somme.

reply, which Paul Baudouin has preserved: "M. Churchill finally declared that he would think over the French requests and reply to them soon. Perhaps a Canadian division might be ready by June 22; perhaps one of the divisions from Dunkirk.

"Fourteen British divisions were being trained, armed only with rifles and machine guns. He intended to draw upon the entire forces of the Empire for:

"eight Indian battalions;

"eight battalions from Palestine;

"14,000 Australians;

"the 2nd Canadian Division;

"one brigade from Narvik.

"But he returned to the necessity of guarding Britain…"

As far as the British land forces were concerned, post-war studies have indeed established these meagre figures as exact. But how sound were Churchill's motives for insisting that R.A.F. Fighter Command must be kept out of the battle for the Somme?

Where was the R.A.F.?

Churchill's supporters have endorsed the view that Britain-would certainly have been invaded in September 1940, if the fighters of the R.A.F. had been sacrificed in the Battle of France. But this viewpoint needs examination. It implies that Churchill was in reality far more pessimistic about the French Army's capacity for resistance than he cared to admit, and that is why he

German artillery unit moving into position at the Battle of The Somme

refused to commit the Spitfires and Hurricanes in France. What are the facts? Could the large-scale intervention of British fighters have turned the scale of the Battle of France?

It could be argued that the total sacrifice of R.A.F. Fighter Command in France would have had punishing effects upon the Luftwaffe. The German air fleets might have suffered such heavy losses that they would have been unable to mount any large-scale air offensives against Britain during the autumn and winter of 1940. Moreover, had the 600-odd fighters at the R.A.F.'s disposal entered the fray, they would have been able to count on the aid of the 350–400 French fighters which were surrendered when the armistice was signed.

Against this, it could be claimed that a transfer to France of R.A.F. Fighter Command would have squandered Britain's trump card. For in France the Spitfires and Hurricanes would have been operating without the benefit of radar, a proper logistical backing and the tactical advantage of operating over their own territory, which gave them a considerable endurance advantage over the Germans in the Battle of Britain.

Shadow of disaster

When he presented his battle plan to the War Committee on May 25, Weygand did not conceal the possibility that the time could well come when the French Army, given only these forces and with no hope of reinforcement, would have suffered such heavy losses that it could no longer hold the Germans. He stressed that it was essential "to stand fast on the present Somme-Aisne line and fight to the last there. This line has several weak points, in particular the Crozat Canal and the Ailette. We could be broken there. If this should happen the surviving fragments will dig in. Every part of the army must fight until it drops for the honour of the country."

It was then that President Lebrun made an intervention which Reynaud has described as "disastrous", but which was natural enough at the time. What would happen, he asked, if the French armies should be scattered and destroyed? In such a crisis the government would have no liberty of action whatsoever, if proposals of peace came from the Germans. True, the agreements made with Britain on March 28 forbade France from concluding a separate peace; but if "relatively advantageous" conditions were offered by the Reich, they should be examined with care. With Reynaud's agreement, Weygand suggested that Britain should be sounded out on every question which would result from the total destruction of the French armies.

After the surrender of Belgium, Weygand once again raised the subject with Reynaud. Listing the reinforcements which France should request from Britain, he added: "It also seems necessary that the British Government be made aware of the fact that a time might come when France would find herself, against her will, unable to continue a military struggle to protect her soil."

It was this possibility which made Reynaud suggest the formation of a "Breton Redoubt". But as we have seen, it would have been impossible for Weygand to withdraw from the line the 12 or so divisions which this would entail. In any case, on June 5 Reynaud made yet another change in his cabinet. Baudouin replaced Daladier as Foreign Minister, Bouthillier replaced

Members of the T0dt constructing a bridge.

Lamoureux as Finance Ministerand Charles de Gaulle, promoted to the temporary rank of brigadier-general, became Under-Secretary for War.

Winston Churchill was born in 1874, the son of a distinguished English politician and an American mother. At Harrow School and at the Royal Military Academy Sandhurst, he displayed little of the brilliance he was to reveal later in many fields.

During his early twenties he gained a reputation as a war correspondent in Cuba, South Africa and (as a serving officer) in India and Egypt; he subsequently became a prolific writer of biography, history, and war memoirs. In India he served on the North-West Frontier, and in Egypt took part in the Battle of Omdurman. In South Africa his escape from a Boer prison camp in 1899 brought him further notoriety. At the age of 26 he entered Parliament. He became Home Secretary in 1910, and First Lord of the Admiralty a year later, resigned in 1915 after the failure of the Dardanelles offensive, but before the war ended was appointed Minister of Munitions. In 1919 he organised the British Expedition against the Bolsheviks. From 1924 to 1929 he was Chancellor of the Exchequer, but all through the thirties he held no office. He became instead a lone voice against British complacency in the face of the rising European dictatorships, and was an untiring campaigner for rearmament. At the outbreak of war he returned to office as First Lord of the Admiralty, and after the fall of the appeaser Neville Chamberlain in May 1940 he was, even at the age of 65, the obvious and popular choice for Prime Minister.

The last act begins

Facing Weygand's 71 divisions, the German commander of Operation "Red" had massed 143 divisions — seven more than on May 10. Three of them had come from the German-Soviet frontier zone, thanks to the benevolent attitude of Stalin and Molotov since the Norwegian campaign. Three others had been diverted from the *Ersatzheer* or training army. And the single infantry division which had been occupying Denmark was also transferred to France. For the coming battle, Hitler and the O.K.W. staff installed themselves in the Belgian village of Brûly-de-Pesche, not far from the O.K.H. headquarters at Chimay.

The French 3rd Army Group was about to be attacked by a new and formidable German concentration under Bock. As the woods and steep gradients of the Chemindes-Dames were unfavourable for armour, the new mass Panzer assault with its usual air support was to be made on the plain of Picardy: Kleist's *Panzergruppe* striking from Péronne and Amiens, and XV Panzer Corps debouching from Longpré, where Rommel's 7th Panzer Division held the railway-bridge. The battle was to rage for 48 hours without the French showing any signs of breaking. In fact, on the evening of June 5 Colonel-General von Bock noted in his war diary: "The French are defending themselves stubbornly."

Certainly, the new tactics which the French were using would not keep the Panzers at bay for long. "For the moment," wrote Hans-Adolf Jacobsen, "[the French tactics] had the following advantage: around Amiens and Péronne, our armoured divisions were able to push their tanks into the gaps between the enemy strongpoints, but our infantry, caught by the flanking fire from the villages, could not follow up. For this reason it was not possible to commit our motorised divisions on the first day."

Strauss' 9th Army, on the Laon sector, also scored mediocre successes on the first day. At Army Group "B" H.Q., the first impression was that this would be a long, hard fight. At Ablaincourt, Captain Jungenfeld, commanding a tank battalion of the 4th Panzer Division, had nine tanks knocked out within minutes. Shortly afterwards his battalion suffered new losses and by noon had only penetrated some 64 miles into the French positions. Jungenfeld described the situation in the following words: "In front of us, every village and wood — one might even say every clump of trees — is literally stuffed with guns and defences; even small artillery detachments can put us under direct fire. Behind us is the glare of a vicious battle where one fights not only for each village, but for each house. We are not therefore surprised to find ourselves under fire from all quarters, and one could say: 'Nobody knows which is the front and which is the rear.'"

And resistance like this was being put up by the French 19th Division, covering seven miles of front and faced by two German corps. On June 6, Bock noted in his diary: "A serious day, rich in crises. It seems that we are in trouble." But at the moment when, "with a heavy heart", he was about to order XIV Motorised Corps to break off the action at Amiens to reinforce the attack of XVI

A German troop carrier passes a line of French POWs.

Panzer Corps, he heard of the successes of his 9th and 4th Armies.

On the left of the German front, 9th Army had thrust across the Chemin des Dames and had reached the Aisne at Soissons. Better still, on the German right, XV Panzer Corps had broken through the French 10th Army, and Rommel's 7th Panzer Division surged forward to Formerie and Forges-les-Eaux on June 7, scattering the 17th Light Division.

This situation forced General Besson to order General Frère to pull back 7th Army into alignment with 6th Army on its right and 10th Army on its left. But this withdrawal amounted to the total sacrifice of the divisions which had defended the line of the Somme so valiantly, and certainly resulted in the loss of most

of their heavy weapons. The 7th Panzer Division, exploiting its successes on the 7th, thrust towards Elbeuf, where the Seine bridges were destroyed at the approach of his first tanks, then swung north-west to reach the Channel at Fécamp. This move trapped General Ihler's IX Corps (which included the French 31st and 40th Divisions and part of the British 51st Division, which had been transferred from the Maginot Line) plus the survivors of 2nd and 5th Light Cavalry Divisions, trapped with their backs to the sea. On June 12, 46,000 French and British troops surrendered at St. Valéry-en-Caux, while 3,300 succeeded in breaking through the German ring.

German forward headquarters of Panzer division on their way to Paris.

France's Agony

On June 9 Rundstedt's Army Group "A" entered the battle against General Requin's 4th Army between Neufchatel and Attigny and the French VII Corps. The French 14th Division fought superbly on the Aisne against the German XXIII Corps. Guderian's Panzergruppe managed to cross the river, however, and the 10th XXXIX Panzer Corps struck out for the south. On June 12 Guderian reached Chalons-sur-Marne. After the battle on the Somme, the battle for Champagne was lost. By June 11 Weygand had only 27 divisions to cover a front of some 280 miles between the Maginot line and the Seine estuary. Weygand ordered the withdrawal to a line Geneva-Dole-Avallon-Cosen (Loire)-Tours-Argentan-Caen-Mouth of the Orne. This longer line was to be covered by only 45 divisions.

On June 10, 1940, Italy went to war, mobilising 73 divisions. Of these 19 were complete, 34 usable, 20 at a state of low efficiency. The Italian divisions were under-strength. The Italian navy had two battleships, 19 cruisers, 126 destroyers and torpedo boats and 117 submarines. Four other battleships were completing trials. However, the fleet was low on oil and had no aircraft carriers. Italy did not have fighter aircraft capable of defending her cities.

In the evening of June 10, on hearing the news that the Germans were crossing the Seine at Andelys and Vernon, President Lebrun and Reynaud's Cabinet left Paris and headed for Tours. Following the example given in 1914 by his predecessor, Myron T. Herrick, U.S. Ambassador William Bullitt stayed

A Frenchman weeps as German soldiers march into the French capital, Paris, on June 14, 1940, after the Allied armies had been driven back across France.

on in Paris. There is a case for the arguments of de Gaulle and the American historian Langer that Bullitt was wrong to do so, for his voice would have carried much weight both in the last French government talks at Bordeaux and in the final inter-Allied discussions. For their part, Generals Weygand and Georges withdrew to Briare with their staffs.

On the 9th, after issuing a vibrant appeal to his troops for continued resistance, Weygand had drawn up a note for the French Government. In it he warned, without yet abandoning hope of stabilising the situation, that the "decisive breakthrough" could come at any moment. He ended: "If this should happen our armies will fight on until they are exhausted, to the last round, but their dispersion will only be a matter of time."

At about 1000 hours on June 10, having listened to the opening paragraphs of Doumenc's report, Weygand sent a note detailing the ever-worsening situation to Reynaud, who had returned to his idea of a "Breton Redoubt" in a directly-argued appeal. Although the word "armistice" had not yet been pronounced, the basic differences between the French Government and High Command were deepening.

The solution to the conflict could have been — and should have been — the replacement of Weygand. Reynaud wanted this, and he had sounded out General Huntziger via de Gaulle, his Under-Secretary for War. According to de Gaulle, Huntziger would have agreed readily if the proposition had been put to him. Henri Massis, however, who was serving at the time in the 4th Army Group, takes the opposite view; and considering the personal friendship between Huntziger and Massis his opinion is probably nearer the mark. The affair went no further, Reynaud deciding to leave things as they were; and this is why (if we replace with "armistice" the word "peace", which he uses incorrectly) de Gaulle was right when he wrote that in taking this decision Reynaud was following "the idea of taking the road of war with a supreme commander who wanted to take the road of peace".

In the meeting of the Supreme War Council held at Briare on the evening of June 11 and on the morning of the 12th, Churchill brought the entire French delegation, including Reynaud, round against him. Resolute and optimistic as to the final outcome of the war, but remote from the actual conflict, he gave a definite "no" to the French request for immediate air aid.

No less than 20–25 British divisions would be fighting beside the French by the following spring; but in the meantime the only British troops in France were the 52nd Division, which had just crossed the Channel, and the 1st Canadian Division, which was disembarking at Brest. A third division would follow on about June 20. At the time of the Briare conference, what more could Churchill offer? It is clear that the R.A.F., entering the fray above the land battles which were developing on the lower Somme and in Champagne, would have been unable to redress the balance, while the French Air Force, left to its own resources, had been largely destroyed as a fighting force. In addition to this, one particular suggestion by Churchill aroused the unanimous opposition of the French leaders: "Will not the mass of Paris and its suburbs present an obstacle dividing and delaying the enemy as in 1914, or like Madrid?"

Quite apart from the fact that Churchill did not apply this argument in the case of the Channel Islands but had them evacuated on the signing of the armistice, his suggestion that Paris be defended was an empty one because neither O.K.H. nor Hitler intended to fight a costly battle for Paris, although this was not known at the French High Command. The French divisions which had been earmarked for the defence of Paris therefore remained inactive, a complete loss to the defence which Weygand was trying to improvise on the Loire.

The day of June 12, when the debate on these grave matters continued, began with a comical incident which might have influenced Churchill's good humour in the morning discussions. According to Benoist-Méchin: "All was calm at the Château du Muguet where Churchill passed the night. Two officers on Weygand's staff were having their breakfast in the dining room (converted into a conference room the day before). Suddenly the door of the room was flung open. In the doorway there appeared a strange sight, a sort of Japanese demon swathed in an ample red silk kimono held in with a white silk belt, a bulky figure with disordered hair who bellowed angrily: 'Uh ay ma bain?'"

It was Churchill, finding that the service in the château left much to be desired. The French officers were paralysed by the apparition and took several moments to recover themselves; but, as the British liaison officer, General Spears, noted: "The Prime Minister, as usual, got his way, and efforts were made to satisfy him." When Spears arrived at Muguet he found Churchill dressing in his room. "He was in a very bad humour."

France: the Fatal Decision

On June 13, Churchill and Lord Beaverbrook met Reynaud at Tours. On June 16 the British Government agreed to France seeking a separate armistice with Germany on the condition that the French sailed forthwith to British harbours. The British also asked for the evacuation of all Polish, Czech and Belgian troops fighting with the French Army. In the event, 24,300 Poles and 5,000 Czechs were embarked for England. After the British proposal for a Franco-British Union had been rejected, Reynaud's Government fell on June 16–17. Pétain formed a new Government on June 16, including Weygand, as Chief of National Defence, and Admiral Darlan, who retained command of the Navy. The new Government agreed an armistice at 0100 hours on the 17th. General de Gaulle flew to London.

The Panzers flood south

At Briare on June 12, Weygand repeated that he hoped to hold on with British help. But on the afternoon of the same day he declared in the French Council: "I will continue to resist, if the Council orders me to do so. But as of this moment I have to make this clear: the ending of hostilities must be considered soon."

On the 13th, driving through the shattered French armies on the lower Somme and in Champagne, the Panzers fanned out in their southward advance: Hoth's group headed for Normandy; Kleist, using the bridges at Nogent and Romilly-sur-Seine, made for the Massif Central and Burgundy; and Guderian swung east, heading for the flank and rear areas of Prételat's 2nd Army Group.

At this point, from the Siegfried Line, Leeb unleashed Operation "Tiger", sending seven divisions from General von Witzleben's 1st Army against the French Saar Detachment under General Hubert. The latter consisted only of General Echard's 52nd Division and General Duch's 1st Polish Division; but despite the fire of 229 artillery batteries and an entire Luftwaffe *Fliegerkorps*, the Germans made no notable progress on the 14th. During the night, however, General Hubert had to retreat in accordance with the order intended to realign 2nd Army Group along the Geneva–Dôle front.

This movement favoured the attack of General Dollmann's German 7th Army which, launching Operation "Bear", crossed the Rhine at Markolsheim and Neuf-Brisach at dawn on the 15th. The XXVII Corps under General Brandt succeeded in gaining only 1¼ miles on the left bank of the Rhine that day, despite the fact that he was faced merely by fortress troops; but further bridging operations by the German sappers allowed 7th Army to expand into the plain of Alsace and to swing towards Mulhouse for a link-up with *Panzergruppe* Guderian.

Although he complains in his memoirs of having been given

A division of Panzer PzKpfw II Moving South.

contradictory orders, Guderian had lived up to the nickname of "Swift Heinz" which his troops had given him. On the evening of the 12th he had been at Châlons-sur-Marne. By noon on the 14th he had reached St. Dizier, which fell to the 1st Panzer Division, urged on by Guderian towards Langres. Langres fell on the 15th, after an advance of 66 miles, and the division pressed on towards Besançon. On June 17 — his 51st birthday — Guderian joined his 29th Motorised Division (which had been advancing on the right of 1st Panzer Division) at Pontarlier on the Swiss frontier. When the news of this exploit came in, Hitler thought that a mistake had been made and that Guderian meant Pontailler-sur-Saône, 50 miles back.

This astonishing raid by XXXIX Panzer Corps indicates clearly enough that after St. Dizier the Germans found no further organised resistance to their advance, apart from some improvised shellfire at the entrances to towns. The same applied to XLI Panzer Corps. Having taken Verdun and Bar-le-Duc on June 15, XLI Corps found itself, 48 hours later, in the region of Vesoul-Port-sur-Saône and Bourbonne-les-Bains. On June 17 an O.K.H. order subordinated *Panzergruppe* Guderian and the 16th Army on its left to Army Group "C". Without losing a moment, the impetuous Guderian swung his Panzer corps through 90 degrees and gave them the following new objectives: XXXIX Panzer Corps —from Pontarlier and Besançon towards Belfort; and XLI Panzer Corps — from Vesoul and Bourbonne-les-Bains towards Epinal and Charmes.

As the 29th Motorised Division was approaching the Swiss frontier, XVI Panzer Corps on the left of *Panzergruppe* Kleist was entering the suburbs of Dijon. The day before, in a battle near Saulieu and Semur-en-Auxois, XVI Panzer Corps had smashed the last resistance put up by the remnants of the French 3rd Armoured Division and by Major-General Maczek's Polish 10th Armoured Brigade, which was fighting its first engagement. As soon as the armistice negotiations began Maczek marched his brigade across France from east to west and embarked it for England. In 1944 he and his compatriots would return to France in the battle for Normandy.

The southward flood of the Panzer advance cut off the line of retreat of all French forces east of the Argonne — 2nd Army Group and the 2nd Army on its left — between Longuyon and Vouziers. General Prételat, who had preceded his troops to their new sector, found himself cut off from them, and General Condé, commander of 3rd Army, took command of this last bastion (if resistance. But before it became clear whether he would break out of the encirclement or fight and die where he stood, a wide gap, some 50 miles across, opened between the Swiss frontier and the Massif du Morvan, clearing the road to Grenoble, Toulon, and Marseilles for the invader.

Similar catastrophe had enveloped the opposite end of the front. On June 16, having reduced the pocket at St. Valéryen Caux, XV Panzer Corps crossed the Seine with Rommel in the van. In front of XV Panzer Corps was 4th Army, whose XXXVIII Corps, led by Manstein, had just reached la Ferté-Vidame, 49 miles south of the bridgehead which he had won. Weygand tried to form a new 10th Army from the survivors of the Somme battle and troops evacuated from Dunkirk, but these forces were mere debris, thrown piecemeal into the fray as soon as they disembarked and lacking all their heavy weapons.

On June 14 the leading troops of the German 18th Army entered Paris, declared an open city and evacuated the day before on the orders of General Héring. His forces, designated the "Army of Paris" had recently been formed between the right of 6th Army and the left of the 7th, both of them now falling back to the Loire.

The Partition of France

At Rethondes on June 24, 1940, France surrendered to Germany. The suspension of hostilities between France, Italy and Germany was set for 0035 hours on Tuesday, June 25. Mussolini's attack on south-eastern France was a failure and threw a blinding spotlight on the weaknesses of Italy's land forces in 1940. The German casualty figures after the battle for France reveal that the Germans suffered much more heavily after Weygand had taken command.

The armistice meant that Germany occupied the industrial northern regions of France while the south was to be left unoccupied under an 'independent' French government. Thanks to the superb fighting skills of the French Army of the Alps, Mussolini's clumsy attempt to overrun south-eastern France was a complete failure.

Should France surrender?

In these conditions — made worse by the refugee exodus and German air attacks — discussions continued between the Allied governments and within Reynaud's Cabinet. It was no longer a question of continuing the fight or of defending metropolitan France: the question now was how to bring about an end of hostilities in conditions which would prove the least damaging for the permanent interests of defeated France.

The debate was still conducted according to the terms of the reciprocal undertakings exchanged by France and Britain in London on March 28, on the occasion of Reynaud's first visit, as Prime Minister, to London. These undertakings pledged the two powers not to conclude any peace treaty or armistice convention without the agreement of the other party. And at Tours on June 13 Churchill gave his formal refusal to release France from the undertaking which she had given.

Certain Frenchmen claimed after the event that as the agreement of March 28 had not been ratified by the French parliament it could not be considered as official. This, surely, is a technical quibble; it was certainly not cited by anyone at the time. But there are no grounds for claiming — as did Reynaud, Georges Mandel, César Campinchi, Jules Jeanneney, Edouard Herriot and others, both at Tours and at Bordeaux — that armistice negotiations blackened the national honour of France. The expression "When matters are impossible, nothing is binding" is not only common sense but a principle of right which is always valid.

In July 1945 the former President of the Republic, Lebrun, was examined as a witness in the trial of Marshal Pétain. His reply to M. Isorni, one of the defence advocates, was unambiguous: "From the moment when one of the two countries which signed

Adolf Hitler in Paris, June 23, 1940.

a convention like that of March 28 retains part of its forces for its own defence, instead of risking it in the common battle — as the British Empire did — it can always keep a paper to recall us to the obligations written on it. But it no longer has the moral authority to say: I will not release you from your obligations."

It is perfectly true that in mid-June 1940 the Hurricanes and Spitfires of the R.A.F., which until then had played only a sporadic part in the battle, represented the main defence of the British Empire; more than that, considering the lack of military preparation of the United States, R.A.F. Fighter Command was in fact the champion of the entire free world, including defeated nations and neutrals. But this does not change the fact that the circumstances of 1940 speak strongly in favour of Lebrun's later argument.

In its appalling situation, with no hope of help from Britain, the French Government therefore had the right to claim its freedom of decision. But this does not necessarily imply that Reynaud's successor made the best decision in preferring an armistice to capitulation.

Armistice or capitulation?

Given this tragic alternative, opinions were divided at the time and remain so today. Hundreds of books have been written on the fall of Reynaud, his replacement by Marshal Pétain, the conclusion of the armistice, and the establishment of the Vichy régime.

A fair analysis can only be made by considering the facts which influenced the key personalities at the time in making their decisions, or the conjectures which could have influenced their reading of the situation. It is misleading, therefore, to refer to documents later discovered in the German archives, which the victors examined after the German surrender in May 1945, in judging the events of June 1940.

While trying to get Weygand to open negotiations with the Germans for the capitulation of the armies entrusted to him, Reynaud wanted to keep the alliance with Britain intact and continue hostilities against Germany. If it crossed to Algiers, his Government would have been able to use the entire French Navy, what could be saved of the Army and Air Force, and the human and material resources of the French Empire. But the counterpart of this plan meant the total surrender of the army-captivity for every man wearing French uniform. And when the Armistice was signed, the Germans announced that they had taken 1,450,000 prisoners. Moreover, Reynaud and his supporters consented to the total occupation of France, not only by the German victors but also by the Italians, who had been unable to make good their claims by force. Finally installed at Toulon, Marseilles, and Port-Vendres, the Axis powers would have been able to carry the war to North Africa.

General Noguès, French C.-in-C. in North Africa, had already been required to send a large proportion of his troops and most of his modern weapons to reinforce the armies in France. On May 20 he had had under his orders 11 infantry divisions, a light division, and two cavalry brigades; a month later he was reduced to eight divisions — three of them territorial — with considerable patrolling and policing duties.

In Libya, Marshal Italo Balbo had mobilised 14 divisions, of which nine were concentrated west of Tripoli. In the west, across the Moroccan frontier, French Intelligence had identified no less than five Spanish divisions, stationed between Ceuta and Larache. How would Spain react if there were no armistice and Hitler decided to carry the war into North Africa? At the very least it seemed that General Franco, who had just occupied Tangier in defiance of international statute, might well open Spain to the passage of the Wehrmacht.

Could the French have reinforced North Africa with troops withdrawn from metropolitan France? This had been thought of, but too late. Nor was this surprising, for according to Navy calculations it would have taken a fortnight to collect sufficient tonnage to transport several hundreds of thousands of men and their equipment. This means that if the project were to have been possible a decision would have had to have been taken around June 1.

On that date it would have been impossible for the French Government to have made the deliberate decision to abandon the whole of France before the crucial battle had been fought — the battle on whose outcome Weygand was far from pessimistic.

In any case, the Germans would have been hard on the heels of the retiring French; and considering the enormous breach which opened on the French right flank, there is every reason to believe that the French defenders of the Loire would have been cut off from the Mediterranean.

The day before the armistice came into being XVI Panzer Corps, which had reached Valence, was ordered by O.K.H. to prepare for an advance against Toulon and Marseilles. At the same time Guderian was ordered to gather his *Panzergruppe* near Montluçon and head for Toulouse, Bordeaux, and the Atlantic coast. Pétain and Weygand were without a shadow of doubt unaware of these orders when they made their decision in favour of an armistice, but a simple look at the map told them that a new encircling move by the Germans could be started at any moment.

The French and Royal Navies could have intercepted any attempts to land Axis troops on the central sector of the Algerian coast; but the bitter experience of Norway had shown that sea power was of no avail in narrow waters without supremacy in the air. It would have been possible for the Spaniards, reinforced by the Germans, to have attacked Morocco across the Strait of Gibraltar, while the Italians, with the aid of the Luftwaffe, attacked Tunis across the Sicilian Channel. As for the numerous French aircraft which landed in Algeria during the last days of the campaign, the question of their supply and replacement only raised new problems.

Faced with all these difficulties, General Noguès ended by rallying, with a heavy heart, to the idea of an armistice. He lamented that American aid had not been requested but at this stage this was more symbolic than real, for Roosevelt's policy had sadly disarmed the United States.

All this reasoning can be criticised on the grounds that Hitler in fact had no intentions of the kind. This is true, but in war one very rarely has the enemy's plans before one, and every possible enemy move must be considered. And the possibility of Hitler choosing to exploit his victory on the far shore of the Mediterranean could not be taken lightly at the time. This was made clear when, on June 19, the Germans asked the beaten French for the use of certain air bases in North Africa and for the authority to set up meteorological bases there. The fact that the request was dropped when the Vichy Government refused to make any concessions of this kind does not make it any the less significant.

Such were the pros and cons of the choice of policy which Reynaud recommended to his colleagues. But he did not fight for it to the bitter end. It seems clear that he had offered his resignation to President Lebrun before the majority of his colleagues had opposed his plans, knowing (none better) that at this crucial moment there was no alternative but an armistice.

First and foremost among the advantages of the latter solution was the fact that a government would be preserved in France at the moment when, invaded, her communications were cut by German air raids and the demolitions of retreating troops, and when 15 per cent of her population consisted of homeless refugees. The appalling fate of Poland, administered by *Reichskommissare* selected for their Nazi Party fanaticism, had become known to the world by 1940. For France in 1940, it seemed better to spare the population a similar fate, despite the rigours of a military occupation which, it was hoped, would apply to as small a part of the country as possible.

Moreover, an armistice would leave France with an army. Certainly, nobody who supported an armistice believed that the victors would leave the French Army the military necessities to resume the struggle with any chance of success. But the example

A German flag flies over Paris.

of the German Army after Versailles spoke for itself. If even a part French Army survived, it could also serve as the basis of future hopes. Meanwhile the Army would demobilise itself, concealing as much war material from the German commissions of inquiry as it could, and retaining the documentation which would make a future remobilisation possible. In addition, in their habitual secrecy, the Intelligence sections of the Army, Navy, and Air Force, together with the counterespionage department, would continue to function.

It was clear that Germany and Italy would not agree to any arrangement which, suspending hostilities in metropolitan France, would not also apply to the fleet and to the Empire. For this reason Weygand, on June 13, had proposed that the fleet be sent to Britain to prevent it falling into enemy hands. This solution had met with the approval of both Churchill and Roosevelt. But how could the French fleet have quitted Toulon, Bizerta, and Mers el Kébir without exposing North Africa, Corsica, and possibly even Provence to Italian naval attacks, and perhaps even landings? This suggestion, too, was rejected by the French Council of Ministers.

Despite all this, even though neutralised, the French Empire and its fleet remained trump cards of the French régime set up after the armistice. If Hitler and Mussolini tried to go too far, they could be made to understand that if they were obdurate the Empire and the fleet would go over to the Allies. This naturally worked the other way. Hitler and Mussolini could make it equally clear that the existence of unoccupied France could depend on the submission of the Empire and the fleet.

Pétain's problems

When Marshal Pétain replaced Reynaud late on June 16, he estimated that the sup porters of an armistice would be outnumbered by those who wanted to continue the war, which meant that the army would eventually have to surrender. But Weygand believed that the honour of the army which he still commanded must prevent him from sending envoys to ask for terms. He had violently rejected similar propositions which Reynaud had made to him, even when the latter had offered to absolve him from responsibility by giving him written orders.

If the choice of an armistice proved to be the less disastrous alternative, one good reason was that General de Gaulle had joined the "dissidents", as they were known during the summer of 1940. Among those who heard de Gaulle's appeal on June 17 — "France has lost a battle! But France has not lost the war!" — were Hitler and Mussolini. German and Italian diplomatic documents prove how attentive they were to every manifestation of "Free France", and this restrained them in the two separate armistice negotiations at Rethondes and the Villa Incisa. Future months would prove this; as Hitler complained to Mussolini in January 1941, without de Gaulle and his Free French, the "Weygand blackmail" would have been much more difficult, if not impossible.

In the meantime, the Axis still had to be persuaded to agree to French rearmament in North Africa.

Benito Mussolini presents his son Bruno with a medal for his services with the Italian Air Corp. in Ethiopia.

Fascist Italy had entered World War II at what seemed to her leaders to be her hour of destiny. But the total and unforeseen collapse of the Allied armed forces resulted in crippling problems for Ciano and Mussolini.

What was Hitler planning next? At the time of the conference at Munich on June 19, Ciano got the impression that Hitler did not wish to risk losing his winnings. If he maintained his current attitude, would he hesitate to sacrifice the international claims of Fascist Italy on the altar of a German-British agreement, to restore the racial solidarity, so to speak, of the Teutonic race? The Italian régime believed that a premature peace settlement would hardly suit Italy's interests, as was proved by the fact that the French-Italian armistice had yielded Mussolini nothing more than Menton and two or three Alpine villages.

But although the Fascist leaders were not eager to see a rapid end to hostilities, they certainly did not want to associate with their German allies in any military ventures upon which Italy might embark in pursuit of her claims in the Balkans and the Mediterranean. This would only have meant offering Hitler a share of the spoils, and as the past history of the Axis had revealed that Germany always desired at least 50 per cent of the cake it is not hard to understand the Italian doubts.

Hitler's contempt for weaker members of the Fascist Party — men like "that swine", as he called Minister of Justice Count Dino Grandi — extended to King Victor Emmanuel III and the House of Savoy, the Pope and the Vatican, and to the entire aristocracy and bourgeoisie of the country. If, as he believed, "traitors" abounded in the most secret councils of his friend Mussolini, there was all the more reason to reveal only the sketchiest hints of his projects to the Duce, and even then to do it as late as possible.

In his distrustful attitude towards Italy Hitler found no opposition from his generals. Quite the contrary: all of them had fought in World War I and remembered what they called Italy's "defection" from the alliance of the Central Powers to the Allied Entente in May 1915. Nor were these professional soldiers in the least impressed by Mussolini's martial swaggering. They strongly suspected that although Fascist Italy's military structure looked impressive, it was built of plaster rather than marble.

As we have seen, the German Army High Command had opposed the suggestion to employ an Italian army in Alsace during the last stage of the Battle of France. While armistice negotiations were still in progress, a suggestion from General Mario Roatta, Deputy Chief-of-Staff of the Italian Army, caused great indignation in his colleague Halder, who noted in his diary on June 24: "The Italians are halted before the French fortifications and are getting nowhere. But in the armistice negotiations they still want to secure an occupied zone of French territory which will be as big as they can get. To this end they have proposed sending to List's front a certain number of Italian battalions to be flown in by air, either by way of Munich or direct to Lyons, and to have them occupy the areas to which Italy wants to extend her right of occupation. All this is nothing more or less than a piece of the most vulgar deception. I have stated that I refused to be associated with the whole business."

Marshal Badoglio, however, also refused to put his name to this sordid project, drawing from Halder the complimentary statement: "According to all appearances, he is the only real soldier among this whole delegation of negotiators."

There can be no doubt that the forthright opinions expressed in Halder's diary were shared by every general close to Hitler and capable of influencing the Führer's decisions.

With all this political and psychological friction there could be no question of the two Axis partners co-ordinating their efforts with a common objective in view, as Britain and the United States would do after Pearl Harbor. Still less was there any chance of creating an Axis counterpart to the Allied Combined Chiefs-of-Staff in Washington, where, although discussions were often acrimonious, the final decisions reached were religiously carried out.

Rome and Berlin therefore followed a system of "parallel war", but with astonishing mutual concealment and even double-dealing. Both General Efisio Marras, for all his title of "Italian Liaison General at O.K.W.", and his opposite number attached to the Comando Supremo, General von Rintelen, were scantily, badly, and tardily informed of the intentions of the two dictator-warlords.

The Germans were understandably incensed when, on October 28, 1940, they found that Mussolini had concealed his intention to invade Greece until the last moment. "Shocking and stupid!" exclaimed Keitel, when he heard the news of the first Italian defeats on the Albanian front. Certainly Keitel had a point, for all the harshness of its expression. But what did Keitel say when Hitler made his decision to make a total reversal of his policy and invade Soviet Russia, without informing Mussolini?

Mussolini and his officers inspect an Italian Air Force squadron and Savoia Marchetti SM81 aircraft.

Germany's anger about Mussolini's Greek campaign is well attested. "In November I went to Innsbruck to meet the German Chief-of-Staff, Marshal Keitel," wrote Badoglio. "He immediately pointed out that we had launched an offensive against Greece without having made the least notification to the German Command. The Führer was adamant that the situation in the Balkans must not be disturbed. Germany was receiving important supplies from those countries, which she now seemed in danger of losing. 'If I had known,' said Keitel, 'I would soon have come to Rome to halt this campaign.'

"I had to tell him the truth, that I had been ordered by Mussolini to say nothing to Germany. He had in fact given me this order, and when I commented that an alliance put certain obligations on us, Mussolini replied furiously: 'Did they ask us anything before attacking Norway? Did they ask our opinion when they wanted to start the offensive in the West? They have acted precisely as if we did not exist. I'll pay them back in their own coin.'"

One would certainly have expected an operation aiming at the conquest of Greece, and above all of the Greek archipelago, to have been on the agenda of Mediterranean strategy at the Brenner Pass conference on October 4, 1940. No operation of the scale of Operation "Barbarossa", the invasion of Russia, was mentioned — a venture which could have been only prejudicial to Italy's interests in the immediate future.

In attacking the Soviet Union, Hitler proposed to deprive Britain of the last ally which she could win on the Continent. But the relaxation of the pressure of the combined forces of the Wehrmacht on Britain could mean only that the joint enemy of the Axis would be able to recover a certain freedom of action.

Such was the system of "parallel war" which Mussolini congratulated himself upon having established against the wishes of his ally and friend. He was confirmed in his euphoria by another factor: when Churchill ignored Hitler's "peace offer" at the end of June 1940, it meant that the war would continue. And as Mussolini said to Badoglio on September 22: "I am happy that the war will not end quickly, for that would be to our total disadvantage. A rapid peace would be a setback for us."

Mussolini, warlord

But again the Duce was forgetting the enormous deficiencies in armaments with which Fascist Italy had gone to war, and the impossibility of making them good in a prolonged war because of Italy's lack of adequate raw materials. It was only a few months since the plain facts had been put before him and he had said to his Chief of the General Staff: "This time I will declare war, but I will not wage it. This way I will get big results for using little effort."

Lybian cavalry charge during display with an Italian officer dressed in white.

On assuming supreme command, however, Mussolini was soon to give the most obvious proof of his lack of military talent. Before his contemporaries, Benito Mussolini, with his strutting stance, jutting chin, hand on hip or thumb hooked in belt, certainly acted the part of a dynamic and resolute commander. Even today, he is represented by the conformist and ill-informed historical viewpoint as a despot who imposed his inexorable will upon the Italian people, after deep and inhuman meditation. But eye-witness accounts and documents show his weathercock nature, his inability to make a decision and stick to it, his lack of method, his ignorance of the basic problems of organisation and command. No Napoleon, in fact.

An important source is the diary of General Quirino Armellini, Badoglio's main colleague at Comando Supremo. Despite the fact that Armellini was opposed to the Fascist régime, the notes which he took between May 11, 1940 and January 26, 1941 — when he was disgraced — are not totally malevolent and tell an eloquent story.

The Alpine offensive had not yet begun when he wrote, on June 21: "The longer I stay at this post, the more I see of the disorder, lack of preparation, and muddle in every sphere, which seriously delay or completely prevent the functioning of the High Command; the more I believe that military necessities are being completely overlooked; and the more I am convinced that everything has yet to be done, or must be done again."

On August 15 he was more bitter still. "What once seemed an interesting prospect today disgusts me! We continue in the greatest disorder and complete chaos. In Comando Supremo, everyone commands. The last man to speak is always right. Strategic conceptions are regularly reversed with an astonishing lack of logic.

"Someone will say: 15 days from now we must be ready to march against Yugoslavia; or, in eight days we will attack Greece from Albania — as easily as saying, let's have a cup of coffee. The Duce hasn't the least idea of the differences between preparing for war on flat terrain or in mountains, in summer or in winter. Still less does he worry about the fact that we lack weapons, ammunition, equipment, animals, raw materials."

Armellini's laments are typical of many, and all would be disastrously confirmed on the battlefield. But when blaming Mussolini and the Fascist régime, how much of the military chaos can be laid at the door of Marshal Badoglio, and, in more general terms, of the Italian Army? In 1946, Badoglio stated that his resignation "would not have resolved the situation", for Mussolini would never have gone back on his pact with Hitler; and Badoglio added: "By retaining my position, I could at least prevent some disastrous move from being made; for this was all which could have been expected from Mussolini, who was completely lacking in any military knowledge."

Badoglio had not invented this explanation to defend himself. On August 15, 1940, he had said to Armellini: "Although it may be a small thing, perhaps I can do more with him than someone else. We must carry on, saving what can be saved, and trying to avoid sudden moves which could lead to more serious consequences."

Writing on St. Helena after Waterloo, Napoleon had thought

Italian submarine in the mouth Bardia Inlet.

very differently. "A commander-in-chief cannot take as an excuse for his mistakes in warfare an order given by his minister or his sovereign, when the person giving the order is absent from the field of operations and is imperfectly aware or wholly unaware of the latest state of affairs.

"It follows that any commander-in-chief who undertakes to carry out a plan which he considers defective is at fault; he must put forward his reasons, insist on the plan being changed and finally tender his resignation rather than be the instrument of his army's downfall."

No sooner, however, had Italy entered the war than setbacks assailed her in all theatres of operations.

The air and sea offensive ordered by Mussolini never truly got under way. What was worse, by June 29 the Italian Navy had lost ten out of the 117 submarines with which it had entered the war, sunk in the Red Sea and the Mediterranean. There was a very good reason for the losses (4 boats) of Italian submarine flotilla based on Massawa in the Red Sea: far too often, when submerged, the accumulator batteries of the submarines gave off poisonous fumes which rendered the crew unconscious.

In Libya, as mentioned above, Marshal Balbo had been ordered to remain on the defensive. If the reports of Comando Supremo's military Intelligence can be taken as correct this was a somewhat odd decision, for 14 centrally-based Italian divisions were opposed by only eight French and five British divisions. But the situation was complicated by an exaggerated interpretation of Allied strength made by the Servizio Informazioni Militari. This did not dissuade Mussolini from going to war, but it did paint the strategic picture in excessively pessimistic colours.

On June 10, 1940, the French C.-in-C., North Africa, General Noguès, did have eight divisions under his command; but apart from the fact that three of them were not operational, they were deployed between the Libyan frontier and Spanish Morocco. The Servizio on the other hand, reported the French divisions as being massed between Bizerta and the Mareth Line, ready for an invasion of Libya. General Sir Archibald Wavell, the British Commander-in-Chief, Middle East, had a total strength of five divisions (about 100,000 men), but of these only 36,000 were in Egypt. They were formed into two incomplete divisions: Major-General M. O'Moore Creagh's 7th Armoured Division and Major-General P. Neame's (from August Major-General N. M. Beresford-Peirse's) 4th Indian Division.

In Libya, the Italian forces were disposed as follows:

West: 5th Army (General Italo Gariboldi), consisting of X, XX, and XXIII Corps, with six infantry divisions and two Black Shirt divisions;

East: 10th Army (General Francesco Berti) consisting of XXI and XXII Corps, with three infantry divisions, one Black Shirt division, and one Libyan native division.

A fourth division (the 2nd Libyan Division) was moving up from Tripoli to Benghazi.

All in all, there were in Italian North Africa slightly over 236,000 officers, N.C.O.'s and other ranks, 1,811 guns, 339 light tanks, 8,039 trucks and 151 first line aircraft. The Italian air strength was comparatively weak, but even so was far stronger than that of the British.

The armistice with France was a bitter disappointment to Marshal Balbo. He had hoped that the occupation of Tunisia would put the port of Bizerta at his disposal, allowing him to draw on the material and military supplies in the province. Instead of this, he had to content himself with the demilitarisation of the Mareth Line.

The Italians were kept off balance for another reason: the British 7th Armoured Division did not imitate the action of the Italian 10th Army and remain on the defensive. Instead, it launched daily armoured and motorised raids across the Libyan frontier, which led the Italians to believe that their weapons were inferior. On June 20 Balbo wrote to Badoglio: "Our light tanks, already old and armed only with machine guns, are completely outclassed. The machine guns of the British armoured cars pepper them with bullets which pierce their armour easily. We have no armoured cars. Our anti-tank defences are largely a matter of make-do; our modern weapons lack adequate ammunition. Thus the conflict has taken on the character of steel against flesh, which only too easily explains certain episodes which are luckily of little importance." There was nothing surprising about the failure of the Italian L-3-33/5 3-ton light tank in Libya, for the "sardine-can", as Franco's men had dubbed it, had cut a sorry figure as early as the Spanish Civil War. One is, however, surprised to read that on June 25 Badoglio announced to Balbo that 70 "magnificent" M-11 tanks were on their way to Libya. In fact this 11-ton tank could be knocked out by any gun with a calibre larger than 20-mm. The standard British anti-tank gun was the 2-pounder (40-mm), and no one in Italy could have been unaware of the fact.

The threat to Egypt

On June 28, on hearing the news that French North Africa would remain loyal to the Government of Marshal Pétain, Comando Supremo ordered Balbo to invade Egypt with his total force, even if this meant "cannibalising" the 5th Army. But Balbo never got the order. On the same day he was shot down over Tobruk by his own gunners during the confusion of an alert.

Marshal Rodolfo Graziani, Army Chief-of-Staff, took over Balbo's command and mission, and D-Day was fixed for July 15, 1940.

In the post which he had just left, Graziani had constantly urged Balbo to take the initiative; but as soon as he arrived in Libya he too began to raise the same arguments against an advance which his predecessor had used. His task was not an easy one. There was only one supply route across the desert between the Libyan frontier and Alexandria, on which were the British bases of Sidi Barrani and Marsa Matrûh. Graziani was not prepared to advance until he had received sufficient trucks and water tankers to supply his transport and the needs of the troops. Moreover, considering the heat of the African summer, he would have preferred to delay the conquest of Egypt until October.

But Mussolini would not hear of this. He wanted to launch the offensive on the same day as the first Germans landed in England. This led to painful scenes between Graziani and Comando Supremo, a visit by Graziani to Rome, and, on August 19, a peremptory telegram from Mussolini which concluded: "Marshal Graziani, as I have already told you since our last discussion, time is working against us. The loss of Egypt will be the coup de grace for Great Britain, while the conquest of that rich country, necessary for our communications with Ethiopia, will be the great reward for which Italy is waiting. That you will procure it, I am certain."

Nevertheless, 10th Army's offensive did not get under way until September 13. Four divisions and an armoured group crossed the frontier, commanded by General Annibale Bergonzoli, C.-in-C. XXIII Corps. Difficult terrain, temperatures at times over 50 degrees Centigrade, sand storms, and anti-tank mines slowed the Italian advance to a bare 122 miles per day. In the afternoon of September 16 the "23rd of March" Black Shirt Division occupied Sidi Barrani. This advance had cost the Italians 120 dead and 410 wounded; the British 7th Armoured Division, which had been ordered to fall back before the advance, had lost 50 men.

In taking Sidi Barrani, Graziani had covered 60 of the 315 miles between the Libyan frontier at Sollum and Alexandria, and was 75 miles from his next objective, Marsa Matrûh. But before moving on Matrûh, Graziani was determined to halt until the damage done by the retreating British had been repaired; until the Via Balbia, the main road which ran across Libya along the coast, had been extended to Sidi Barrani, where the road to Alexandria began; to set up a fresh-water pipeline; and to stock Sidi Barrani with provisions, ammunition, and fuel. Graziani, a veteran colonial general, was entirely correct in taking all these precautions, for Wavell was hoping to see the Italian forces over-extend themselves by a premature dash on Matrûh.

Mussolini was disappointed by the pause in the offensive. But he consoled himself by reflecting that although the Italians had not passed Sidi Barrani, the Germans had not crossed the Channel.

Hitler restrains Mussolini

Mussolini had nobody but himself to blame for the

sluggishness and delays of Graziani. If Mussolini had not kept the greater part of the resources which had been released by the Franco-Italian armistice in Italy, things might have turned out very differently during the invasion of Egypt. But at the beginning of July he had decided to smash Yugoslavia, that "creation of Versailles" which had to disappear like the others.

As a result three armies, totalling some 37 divisions, were concentrated in north-eastern Italy. But Hitler was anxious that peace should not be disturbed in this corner of the Continent. On August 17 Ribbentrop, via Ambassador Dino Alfieri, informed

Italian vessel Bartolomeo Colleoni sinking after an attack from the HMS Sydney.

Ciano of the Führer's opposition to any venture against Yugoslavia or Greece. Mussolini had to yield, but what was he to do with the armies which were now left without a mission? For reasons of economy, 600,000 soldiers were demobilised and sent home, to be remobilised a few weeks later.

In the summer of 1940, as far as circumstances permitted, the maritime honours went to the Royal Navy, which more than lived up to its aggressive tradition.

Is it fair to blame the Italian admirals for their lack of offensive spirit? They were certainly kept on a far shorter rein by the Italian High Command in Rome — Supermarina — than were their opponents. But one reason for Supermarina's reticence was the early realisation that the Italian Air Force was not to be relied upon, whether for reconnaissance missions or for combat.

This was shown clearly during the action off Cape Spartivento on the Calabrian coast on July 9, 1940. The Italian fleet, under Admiral Campioni, was returning to base after having escorted an important convoy carrying troops and material to Benghazi. The British Mediterranean Fleet, under Admiral Cunningham, was also at sea; it was well informed about the movements of the Italian fleet, by aircraft operating from Malta and from the aircraft-carrier Eagle; and Cunningham planned to intercept . the Italians during their return to Taranto.

Cunningham did not succeed, but the battleship Warspite managed to hit the Italian battleship Giulio Cesare at a range of 26,000 yards. Campioni broke away under the cover of a smoke screen, and Cunningham, having closed to within 25 miles of the Italian coast, also withdrew. On this occasion the Italian Air Force showed all its weaknesses; no dive-bombing or torpedo attacks were made during the encounter, and only one of the 1,000 bombs dropped scored a hit - on the cruiser Gloucester.

This inaccuracy did have its good side: it spared the Italian fleet from heavy losses, when Campioni's ships were enthusiastically bombed by the Savoia-Marchetti 79's of the Italian Air Force. On July 13 Ciano noted in his diary: "The real controversy in the matter of naval armament is not between us and the British, but between our Air Force and our Navy."

Nevertheless, Mussolini announced with a straight face that within three days half the British naval potential in the Mediterranean had been eliminated. On July 19 there was another encounter in the Antikithera Channel off the northwest coast of Crete. The Italian light cruisers Bartolomeo Colleoni and Bande Nere, which were heading for Leros in the Dodecanese, fell in with the Australian light cruiser Sydney and five destroyers. Hit in her engine-rooms, the Colleoni was immobilised and sunk by torpedoes, while the Bande Nere escaped. This was a clear indication of combat weaknesses of these light warships, in which protection had been sacrificed for the sake of speed.

In early August, however, the naval balance in the Mediterranean appeared to shift heavily in Italy's favour. The battleships Littorio, Vittorio Veneto, Caio Duilio, and Andrea Doria joined the Italian fleet. The first two were powerful, modern warships displacing over 41,000 tons, with a main armament of nine 15-inch guns and a top speed of 28 knots. The others were battleships which had been launched in 1913 and completely overhauled in the late 1930's. The two Doria-class battleships were each armed with ten 12.6-inch guns and could make 26 knots.

From its central position this formidable battle fleet outnumbered the combined squadrons of Admirals Somerville and Cunningham by six capital ships to five, the British squadrons being separated at opposite ends of the Mediterranean. The British still had a slight advantage in firepower, but none of the battleships in the Mediterranean Fleet was faster than 24 knots. After the affair off Calabria, the British Admiralty sent to the eastern Mediterranean the battleship Valiant (fresh from a refit), the anti-aircraft cruisers Calcutta and Coventry, and, most important of all, the new aircraft-carrier Illustrious, which carried 34 aircraft, of which 12 were Fulmar fighters. With this reinforcement Cunningham's battle fleet could defend itself adequately against the Italian bombers. Illustrious and Valiant had the additional advantage of being equipped with radar.

Thus the Royal Navy had reacted promptly and skilfully: these new reinforcements anchored at Alexandria on September 5.

During the operation the veteran aircraft-carrier Argus, having steamed to the south of Sardinia, flew off 12 Hurricanes to strengthen the threadbare defences of Malta. It is surprising to note that after the neutralisation of Bizerta with the signing of the armistice, the Italians had made no attempt to take Malta. The defences of the "island fortress" were pitifully weak: there were only 68 light and heavy A.A. guns instead of the 156 guns which had been envisaged in a pre-war programme, and the one radar set on the island functioned only sporadically. When Italy entered the war on June 10 Malta's air defences consisted of five Swordfish torpedo-bombers and four Sea Gladiators; one of the latter was soon damaged beyond repair, and the remaining three were christened "Faith", "Hope", and "Charity". These were later joined by nine Swordfish and nine Hurricanes.

Admiral Cunningham had protested against the running-down of Malta's defences which the British Government and the Imperial General Staff had countenanced, but his complaints had not been taken up. London had decided that in the event of a war with Italy the Middle East theatre would be supplied by the sea route round the Cape of Good Hope. But in view of the timidity of Comando Supremo and the weaknesses of the Italian Air Force it was decided to restore to Malta the offensive rôle which had seemed impossible because of the menace of the bomber.

But to do this it would be necessary to proceed by very careful and easy stages while the defences of the island remained as weak as they were. Cunningham saw this very clearly. He wrote at the time: "If we are to avoid a serious threat to Malta itself, it appears necessary that in any given period the scale of attack drawn down should not be disproportionate to the state of the defences it has been possible to install. It is only logical therefore to expect the full weight of Italian attack if our light forces work effectively."

In the long run, the offensive action of the light surface forces and the bombers which would be based on Malta would depend on the parallel development of Malta's defences (fighters, anti-aircraft guns, and radar). This was obvious; it was confirmed by experience. But it did not appeal to Churchill, who reproached Cunningham on September 9 for not being sufficiently offensively minded.

Meanwhile, a local conflict with no direct connection with the war between the major powers was about to become a matter of great importance. Soon it would impinge upon the joint interests of Germany and Italy — with fateful results.

We have already mentioned that neither the Hungarian Regent, Admiral Horthy, the various governments at Budapest, nor Hungarian national opinion had accepted the territorial restrictions imposed upon Hungary by the Treaty of Trianon in 1920. After Munich, Hungary had obtained substantial frontier rectifications at the expense of Czechoslovakia; later, in March 1939, the Prague coup had enabled her to occupy and annex Sub-Carpathian Ruthenia. But Hungary had other claims to make, against both Yugoslavia and Rumania.

For many years the region of Transylvania had been a source of discord between Rumania and Hungary. With the defeat of Austria-Hungary in 1918, Hungary had been forced to cede Transylvania to Rumania, the latter country being one of the victorious Allies. It was a fair enough decision, considering that the majority of the population was Rumanian and that it had endured harsh treatment while under Hungarian rule. But along the bend of the Carpathians there was a compact bloc of Magyars, known as Szeklers or Sicules. There were around two million of them, and they were cut off from their fellow Magyars on the Danubian plain. When they became Rumanian citizens, they had no reason to be pleased with their change of nationality.

The Axis verdict

After the crushing of France, the Hungarian Government once again raised the question of Transylvania. But although King Carol II of Rumania and his Prime Minister, Gigurtu, were prepared to consider certain concessions, no complete agreement between the rival countries seemed possible. They would have gone to war but for the intervention of Hitler, who, as we have seen, feared the consequences of any outbreak of trouble in the Balkans, and Mussolini, who always tended to favour the cause of the Hungarians. Rumania and Hungary submitted to Axis arbitration, which was presided over by Ciano and Ribbentrop in the Belvedere Palace in Vienna. On August 30, 1940, the Axis verdict was delivered.

Under the terms of the Axis arbitration, Rumania would retain the western part of Transylvania. Hungary recovered the region of the Szeklers, but in order to extend her 1920 frontier to the Moldavian Carpathians she was also granted territory occupied by some three million Rumanians, plus the important towns of Cluj and Oradea, which for the next four years were known by the Magyar names of Kolozsvar and Nagyvárad.

This high-handed partition of Transylvania still did not satisfy the Hungarian claims in full. On the other hand, coming as it did two months after the loss of Bessarabia and the Bukovina to Soviet Russia, it sparked off deep feelings of resentment among the Rumanians. On September 4 General Ion Antonescu seized power, forced King Carol to abdicate in favour of his son Prince Michael, and, taking the title of "Conducator", set up a dictatorship.

British in occupation at Italian Somaliland by a monument which stands on the equator.

German patronage for Rumania

As Italy, of the two Axis partners, had always supported Hungary's cause, it was not surprising that both King Carol and Antonescu had thought it advisable to seek German patronage. Hitler was extremely anxious not to be cut off from the output of the Rumanian oil wells at Ploie ti, and to safeguard them from possible Allied attempts at sabotage. As a result, he welcomed eagerly the request made to him by a Rumanian military mission which visited him on September 2. And on October 7, Lieutenant-General Hansen and his staff, together with the first elements of the 13th Motorised Division, arrived in Bucharest.

This move, coming as it did after the guarantee of territorial integrity which had been given to Rumania after the Vienna arbitration, could only be interpreted as a clear-cut anti-Soviet move by Hitler. Stalin and Molotov, however, showed no outward reaction. But the effect on Mussolini was totally different.

Admiral Miklos Horthy de Nagybánya was born in 1868 in eastern Hungary. When 14 he entered the Austro-Hungarian naval academy. Between 1909 and 1914 Horthy was the Emperor Franz Joseph's naval aide-de-camp, and during World War I was noted as a daring and able leader. He was promoted Admiral in January 1918. After the war Horthy returned to Hungary and led the counterrevolution which ousted the Communists from power. He became Regent in March 1920, but refused to surrender the office in 1921. His policies were based on a desire to maintain the current social order and extend Hungary's borders. Though on bad terms with Hitler, Horthy joined the Axis in 1941, chiefly so that he could continue his struggle against Communism. He tried

Field Marshall Rommel with Benito Mussolini.

to secure a separate peace in 1944, but was imprisoned by the Nazis. He died in Portugal in 1957.

Mussolini turns on Greece

On October 12 Ciano visited Mussolini in the Palazzo Venezia. He found the Duce "indignant", claiming that the occupation of Rumania by German troops had had a very bad impression on Italian public opinion. He had made his decision. "Hitler always faces me with a fait accompli. This time I am going to pay him back in his own coin. He will find out from the papers that I have occupied Greece. In this way the equilibrium will be re-established."

No other decision of Mussolini's could have been more welcome to Ciano, who had always pressed for imperialist Italian policies in the eastern Mediterranean. Nevertheless he thought it necessary to ask if Mussolini had discussed the matter with Marshal Badoglio. "Not yet," he replied, "but I shall send in my resignation as an Italian if anyone objects to our fighting the Greeks."

On the 15th Badoglio and Roatta, appalled, heard of Mussolini's decision. Three weeks before, acting on his orders, they had demobilised 600,000 men. Now he was asking them to attack Greece within 12 days, D-Day being set as dawn on October 26.

Without objecting to the operation in principle, Badoglio undertook to attack with 20 Italian divisions on condition that the Bulgarians would undertake to tie down six to eight Greek divisions. But General Sebastiano Visconti-Prasca, commanding in Albania, only had eight Italian divisions under his orders. It would therefore be necessary to remobilise 12 more divisions, send them across the Adriatic, and set up the necessary depôts and reserves for them on the spot. Considering the inadequacies of the Albanian ports of Valona and Durazzo, all this needed at least three months.

Mussolini could not accept these arguments: everything suggested that such a delay would allow Hitler to interpose a new veto. Ciano, Jacomoni (LieutenantGeneral of Albania), and Visconti-Prasca all supported the idea. During the discussions on October 15 at the Palazzo Venezia they destroyed the objections of Badoglio and Roatta; and they were backed by Admiral Cavagnari and General Pticolo, respectively Under-Secretary of State and Chief-of-Staff of the Navy, and Chief-of-Staff of the Air Force.

As Ciano saw it, the political situation was favourable. Neither Turkey nor Yugoslavia would support Greece, their ally in the Balkan Pact, and Bulgaria's attitude would be favourable to Italy. But above all, the political situation in Athens gave cause for reasonable optimism. Only the Court and the plutocracy remained hostile to Fascist Italy, and a well-organised system of bribery was laying the groundwork for a change of régime.

For his part, Jacomoni claimed that the entire population of Albania was anxious to settle accounts with Greece, its hereditary enemy. "One can even state," he declared proudly, "that the enthusiasm is so great that it [the Albanian people] has recently given signs of disillusionment that the war has not already begun."

Asked to present his plan of operations, Visconti-Prasca declared that he foresaw no difficulty in opening the campaign with his current forces in Albania. Leaving a covering force on the Pindus Mountains on the eastern sector, he undertook to conquer Epirus in 10 to 15 days, throwing 70,000 Italians against 30,000 Greeks. Then, reinforced from Italy and from the Ionian Islands through the captured port of Préveza, he would march on Athens, whose fall would end the campaign before the close of the year.

Faced with these arguments, particularly the political explanations of Ciano and Jacomoni, Badoglio gave way. He contented himself with saying that the Peloponnese and Crete should be included as objectives, for otherwise the British would move in. He has been blamed correctly — for the exaggerated military promises which he made. But at the time he had no idea of the extent to which the claims of Ciano and Jacomoni were totally mistaken.

Nevertheless, Mussolini granted his generals a deadline extension of two days; and he impressed on all parties that the whole affair was to be kept a strict secret from the Germans.

Hitler and the Mediterranean

While the preliminary studies for an invasion of Soviet Russia were still under way, Hitler, on the urging of Grand-Admiral Raeder and the suspension of Operation "Sea Lion", was showing signs of interest in a strategic project which could have lessened the weakening effects of the "parallel war" and allowed the Axis partners to co-operate more directly in their fight against the common enemy. This was Operation "Felix", aimed at the

Italian troops at Amba Alagi.

conquest of Gibraltar.

If the Wehrmacht could establish itself on the Strait of Gibraltar it could close the Mediterranean to the Royal Navy and give the Italian fleet access to the Atlantic. It would also enable the Axis to put French North Africa, where Weygand had just installed himself, under pressure similar to that already being imposed on Unoccupied France. It would no longer be possible for Vichy France to fend off Hitler's demands by pleading the possible defection of Morocco, Algeria, and Tunisia.

Overtures to Franco

Such an operation would require the cooperation of Spain. When it seemed likely that Hitler was about to invade Britain, the Spanish Government had raised the question of Spain's claims to Oran and the French zone of the Moroccan protectorate. In mid-September Serrano Suñer, Spanish Minister of the Interior and Franco's brother-in-law, met Hitler and Ribbentrop for a series of talks. According to his account, which, it is true, was written after the war, he was disappointed — not to say shaken — by the German reaction to these overtures.

Ciano's diary confirms Suñer's version. On October 1 it records "Serrano's colourful invectives against the Germans for their absolute lack of tact in dealing with Spain. Serrano is right."

Hitler and Ribbentrop wanted the Atlantic coast of Morocco for Germany, plus an air and naval base in the Canary Isles. Moreover, they were still uncertain about the economic aid which Germany could send to Spain, for the moment she entered the war Spain would instantly be cut off from her important imports of cereals and fuel, and would then become dependent on Germany.

On October 4 the same question was raised at the Brenner Pass conference between Hitler, Mussolini, Ribbentrop, and Ciano. At the same time the eventual dispatch of a German armoured detachment to North Africa was discussed. But Mussolini, who was still waiting from day to day for Graziani to resume his offensive in Egypt, cold-shouldered the idea. In his opinion, Panzer troops should only be sent to North Africa after the third phase of the operation: when the Italian 10th Army moved east from Marsa Matrûh on Alexandria and Cairo. There can be no doubt, however, that he hoped to be able to avoid German help.

If the Italians had taken Cairo by October 22, Franco could well have acted very differently. As it was, on that day he met Hitler at Hendaye on the Spanish frontier. Franco believed that the war would in fact be a long one and that without firm guarantees of corn and fuel supplies it would only impose further bitter sacrifices on the Spanish people.

As Hitler continued to speak in general terms, affirming that Britain was already beaten, Franco turned down the invitation to enter the war on the day that the Wehrmacht attacked Gibraltar, provisionally set for January 10, 1941.

Interpreter Paul Schmidt was an eyewitness at this discussion.

"To put it bluntly, I was most interested to hear Franco's reply to Hitler's declaration that from the jumping-off point of Gibraltar, Africa could be rid of the British by armoured troops." This was quite possible along the fringe of the great desert, said Franco, "but central Africa is protected against any large-scale land offensive by the desert belt, which defends it as the sea defends an island. I have fought a great deal in Africa and I am certain of it."

Schmidt's account continues: "Even Hitler's hopes of eventually conquering Britain might turn out to be hollow. Franco thought it possible that the British Isles could be conquered. But if this happened the British Government and fleet would carry on the struggle from Canada, with American aid.

"While Franco talked on in a calm, monotonous, sing-song voice like an Arabic muezzin, Hitler began to grow more and more restless. The discussion was clearly fraying his nerves. At one stage he even got up and said that further discussion would be useless, but he soon sat down and continued his attempt to change Franco's mind. Franco declared that he was prepared to conclude a treaty but, in view of the supplies of food and armaments Hitler was prepared to offer from the moment Spain went to war, that the offer was only a hollow sham."

Franco was using the technique which can loosely be described as "yes, but", and it was not at all to the liking of Hitler. Ribbentrop, too, was receiving the same treatment from Serrano Suñer, who had only lately become the Spanish Minister of Foreign Affairs. Ribbentrop's latest proposal had not been well received by Suñer: "Spain will receive territories from the French colonial empire, for which France can be compensated in equal measure by territories from the British colonial empire."

This was very different to what had been said to Suñer during his visit to Berlin; but Ribbentrop, too, was infuriated by the caution of the Spaniards. Schmidt, who flew to Montoire with Ribbentrop, has described him as "fuming with rage", and spending the journey in invective against "that ungrateful rogue" Franco and "that Jesuit" Suñer.

Pétain refuses to help Hitler

If Hitler's meeting with Franco at Hendaye was a definite setback for German policies, his meeting with Pétain at Montoire did nothing to compensate for it. Hitler wanted to induce the Vichy French Government to go to war with Britain. Pétain, however, left Hitler in no doubt as to his refusal to allow France to be drawn into a war with her former ally, even on the pretext of reconquering the colonies which had gone over to de Gaulle.

Once again, Schmidt has provided an account of the Montoire meeting.

"As darkness fell on October 24, 1940, it was difficult at first to tell the victor from the vanquished in the feeble lights on the platform of the little station. Standing very straight, despite his great age, in his plain uniform, Pétain put out his hand to the dictator with an almost royal gesture, while fixing him with a quizzical, icy, and penetrating glance. I knew how he felt about Hitler, Göring, and other prominent National Socialists. To most Germans he himself stood for all the military virtues of France, and this was very clear in Hitler's attitude when they met. He was no longer the triumphal victor shown by certain photographs

of 1940. Nor was he a corporal intimidated in the presence of a marshal, as certain French publications have since claimed. He behaved without haughtiness and without harshness.

"With a gesture, Hitler invited the Marshal to enter his railway car. I myself was seated before Pétain and was admirably placed to observe him throughout the talk. His complexion, which had seemed pale to me on the platform, became faintly pink. No emotion or interior tension could be seen behind his mask of impassivity. Ribbentrop, a mute and almost tolerated witness, together with Laval, who was wearing his inevitable white tie, assisted the conversation.

"Pétain listened in silence. Not once did he offer a single friendly word for Hitler or for Germany. His attitude conveyed a vaguely haughty impression, rising above the situation of France in this autumn of 1940."

CHRONOLOGY OF WORLD WAR II

	1938
March 11	Anschluss — German annexation of Austria.
September 29	Munich Agreement signed.
October 5	Germany occupies Sudetenland.
	1939
March 14	Slovakia declares its independence.
March 31	Britain and France give guarantee to Poland.
April 7	Italy invades Albania.
May 22	Germany and Italy sign Pact of Steel.
August 23	Molotov-Ribbentrop pact signed between Germany and the Soviet Union.
September 1	Germany invades Poland.
September 1	Britain and France declare war on Germany.
September 17	Soviet Union invades Poland.
November 30	Soviet Union at war with Finland.
	1940
March 12	War between Soviet Union and Finland ends.
April 9	Germany invades Norway and Denmark.
April 14	Allied troops land in Norway.
May 10	Fall Gelb, the offensive in the West, is launched by Germany.
May 10	Churchill becomes Prime Minister of Great Britain.
May 14	Dutch Army surrenders.
May 26	Beginning of evacuation of Dunkirk.
May 28	Belgium surrenders.
June 2	Allies withdraw from Norway.
June 4	Dunkirk evacuation complete.
June 10	Italy declares war on Britain and France.
June 14	Germans enter Paris.
June 21	Italy launches offensive against France.
June 22	France and Germany sign armistice.
June 24	France and Italy sign armistice.
July 3	Royal Navy attacks French fleet at Mers el Kebir.
July 10	Beginning of the Battle of Britain.
September 17	Operation Sealion (the invasion of England) postponed by Hitler.
September 21	Italy and Germany sign Tripartite Pact.
September 27	Japan signs Tripartite Pact.
November 20	Hungary signs Tripartite Pact.
November 22	Romania signs Tripartite Pact.
November 23	Slovakia signs Tripartite Pact.
	1941
January 19	British launch East African campaign offensive.
January 22	Australian troops take Tobruk.
February 6	British capture Benghazi.
February 11	Rommel arrives in Libya.

March 25	Yugoslavia signs Tripartite Pact.
March 27	Yugoslavia leaves Tripartite Pact after coup d'etat.
March 28	Successful British naval action against Italians off Cape Matapan.
April 6–8	Axis forces invade Yugoslavia and Greece.
April 11	U.S.A. extends its naval neutrality patrols.
April 13	Belgrade falls to Axis forces.
April 14	Yugoslav forces surrender.
April 22	Greek First Army surrenders at Metsovan Pass.
May 16	Italians surrender to British at Amba Alagi.
May 20	Germans land on Crete.
May 24	H.M.S. Hood sunk by Bismarck.
May 27	Bismarck sunk by Royal Navy.
June 1	British withdraw from Crete.
June 2	Germany launches Operation Barbarossa against the Soviet Union.
July 27	Japanese troops invade French Indo-China.
September 19	Germans capture Kiev.
September 28	Three-power Conference in Moscow.
December 6	Britain declares war on Finland, Hungary and Rumania.
December 7	Japanese attack Pearl Harbor.
December 8	U.S.A. and Britain declare war on Japan.
December 8	Japanese invade Malaya and Thailand.
December 11	Germany and Italy declare war on the U.S.A.
December 14	Japanese begin invasion of Burma.
December 25	Japanese take Hong Kong.
1942	
February 15	Japanese troops capture Singapore from British.
February 27	Battle of the Java Sea.
February 28	Japanese invade Java.
March 8	Japanese invade New Guinea.
March 17	General MacArthur appointed to command South-West Pacific.
April 9	U.S. troops surrender in Bataan.
April 16	George Cross awarded to Island of Malta by H.R.H. King George VI.
April 26	Anglo-Soviet Treaty signed.
May 6	Japanese take Corregidor.
May 7	Battle of the Coral Sea.
May 20	British troops withdraw from Burma,
May 26	Rommel's Afrika Korps attack British at Gazala.
May 30	Royal Air Force launches first thousand-bomber raid on Germany.
June 4	Battle of Midway.
June 21	Rommel's Afrika Korps take Tobruk.
July 1	Sevastopol taken by Germans.
July 1	First Battle of El Alamein.
August 7	U.S. troops land on Guadalcanal.
August 11	PEDESTAL convoy arrives in Malta.
August 19	Raid on Dieppe.

August 31	Battle of Alam Halfa.
October 24	Second Battle of El Alamein.
November 8	Operation TORCH landings in North Africa.
November 11	Germans and Italians occupy Vichy France.
November 27	French fleet scuttled at Toulon.
1943	
January 14–24	Allied Conference at Casablanca.
January 23	British troops take Tripoli.
February 2	Germans surrender at Stalingrad.
February 8	Red Army captures Kursk.
February 13	Chindits launch first operation into Burma.
February 19	Battle for the Kasserine Pass.
April 19	First Warsaw rising.
April 19	Bermuda Conference.
May 11–25	TRIDENT conference in Washington.
May 13	Axis forces surrender in North Africa.
May 16	Royal Air Force "Dambuster" raid on Mohne and Eder dams.
May 24	U-boats withdraw from North Atlantic.
July 5	Battle of Kursk.
July 10	Allies land in Sicily.
July 25	Mussolini resigns.
September 3	Allies land on Italian mainland.
September 8	Surrender of Italy announced.
September 9	Allies land at Salerno.
September 10	Germans occupy Rome and Northern Italy.
October 13	Italy declares war on Germany.
November 6	Red Army captures Kiev.
November	First Allied conference in Cairo. 23–26
November 28–December 1	Allied conference in Teheran.
December 3–7	Second Allied conference in Cairo.
December 24	General Eisenhower promoted to supreme commander for OVERLORD, the Normandy landings.
1944	
January 22	Allies land at Anzio.
January 27	Red Army raises Siege of Leningrad.
January 31	U.S. forces land on Marshall Islands.
February 1	Battle for Monte Cassino begins.
March 2	Second Chindit operation into Burma.
May 11	Fourth Battle of Monte Cassino.
June 4	U.S. troops enter Rome.
June 6	Operation OVERLORD — Allied landings in Normandy.
June 19	Battle of the Philippine Sea.
July 1	Breton Woods conference.
July 20	Failed attempt to assassinate Hitler — July Bomb plot.
August 1	Second Warsaw rising.
August 4	Allied troops enter Florence.

August 15	Operation DRAGOON — Allied landings in southern France.
August 25	Germans in Paris surrender.
September 4	British troops capture Antwerp.
September	OCTAGON — Allied conference at Quebec. 12–16
September 17	Operation MARKET GARDEN at Arnhem.
September 21	Dumbarton Oaks conference.
October 14	British enter Athens.
October 23	De Gaulle recognised by Britain and U.S.A. as head of French Provisional Government.
October 24	Battle of Leyte Gulf.
December 16	Germans launch campaign in the Ardennes.
1945	
January 4–13	Japanese Kamikaze planes sink 17 U.S. ships and damage 50 more.
January 14	Red Army advances into East Prussia.
January 17	Red Army takes Warsaw.
January 30–February 3	First ARGONAUT Allied conference at Malta.
February 4–11	Second ARGONAUT Allied conference at Malta.
February 6	Allies clear Colmar pocket.
February 19	U.S. forces land on Iwo Jima.
February 26	U.S. 9th Army reaches Rhine.
March 7	U.S. 3rd Army crosses Rhine at Remagen Bridge.
March 20	British capture Mandalay.
March 30	Red Army enters Austria.
April 1	U.S. First and Ninth Armies encircle the Ruhr.
April 1	U.S. forces land on Okinawa.
April 12	President Roosevelt dies and Truman becomes president.
April 13	Red Army takes Vienna.
April 25	U.S. and Soviet forces meet at Torgau.
April 28	Mussolini shot by partisans.
April 29	Germans sign surrender terms for troops in Italy.
April 30	Hitler commits suicide.
May 2	Red Army takes Berlin.
May 3	British enter Rangoon.
May 4	German forces in the Netherlands, northern Germany and Denmark surrender to General Montgomery on Luneburg Heath.
May 5	Germans in Norway surrender.
May 7	General Alfred Jodl signs unconditional surrender of Germany at Reims, to take effect on May 9.
May 8	Victory in Europe Day.
May 10	Red Army takes Prague.
July 17–August 2	Allied TERMINAL conference held in Potsdam.
July 26	Winston Churchill resigns after being defeated in the general election. Clement Attlee becomes Prime Minister of Great Britain.
August 6	Atomic bomb dropped on Hiroshima.
August 8	Soviet Union declares war on Japan.
August 9	Atomic bomb dropped on Nagasaki.
August 14	Unconditional surrender of Japanese forces announced by Emperor Hirohito.
August 15	Victory in Japan Day.
September 2	Japanese sign surrender aboard U.S.S. Missouri in Tokyo Bay.